KB239078

NE능률
영어교과서

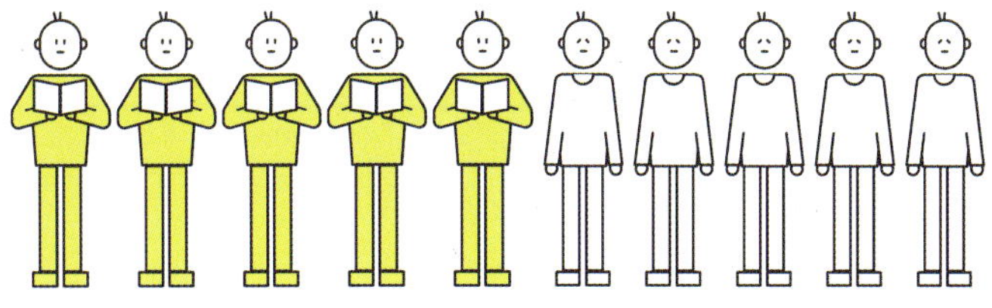
대한민국 고등학생 10명 중
4.7명이 보는 교과서
영어 고등 교과서 점유율 1위
(7차, 2007 개정, 2009 개정, 2015 개정)

READING TUTOR
리딩튜터
그동안 판매된
리딩튜터 1,700만 부
차곡차곡 쌓으면 17만 미터
에베레스트
19배 높이
170,000m
에베레스트 8,848m

능률보카
그동안 판매된
능률보카 1,000만 부
대한민국 박스오피스
천만명을 넘은 영화
단 23개
VOCA

그래머존
그동안 판매된 330만 부의 그래머존을 바닥에 쭉 ~ 깔면
900km 서울-부산 왕복가능
서울
부산

초등
Grammar
Inside 6

지은이	NE능률 영어교육연구소
선임연구원	김지현
연구원	송민아, 김준희
영문교열	Curtis Thompson, Angela Lan, Olk Bryce Barrett
디자인	안훈정
내지 일러스트	김주명, 곽호명, 박응식
맥편집	권재희
영업	한기영, 이경구, 박인규, 정철교, 김남준, 김남형, 이우현
마케팅	박혜선, 고유진, 김여진
Photo Credits	Shutterstock

NE능률이 미래를 그립니다.

교육에 대한 큰 꿈을 품고 시작한 NE능률
처음 품었던 그 꿈을 잊지 않고 40년이 넘는 시간 동안 한 길만을 걸어왔습니다.

이제 NE능률이 앞으로 나아가야 할 길을 그려봅니다.
'평범한 열 개의 제품보다 하나의 탁월한 제품'이라는
변치 않는 철학을 바탕으로 진정한 배움의 가치를 알리는
NE능률이 교육의 미래를 열어가겠습니다.

NE 능률
www.neungyule.com

초등
Grammar
Inside

6

# 구성 및 활용법

<table>
<tr><td>**STEP 1** 문법 개념 확인</td><td>▶</td><td>**STEP 2** 연습 문제</td></tr>
<tr><td>쉽고 간단한 문법 설명과 시각적으로 잘 정리된 표를 통해 문법 개념을 빠르게 익혀요.</td><td></td><td>간단한 확인 문제부터 문장 완성까지 다양한 유형과 난이도의 문제로 배운 문법을 적용해요.</td></tr>
</table>

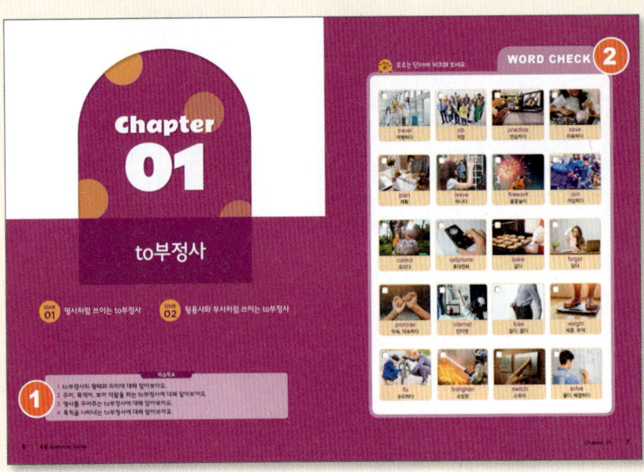

❶ 학습목표

해당 Chapter에서 배울 내용을 미리 예측해 볼 수 있어요.

❷ WORD CHECK

Chapter에 등장할 단어를 미리 학습할 수 있어요.

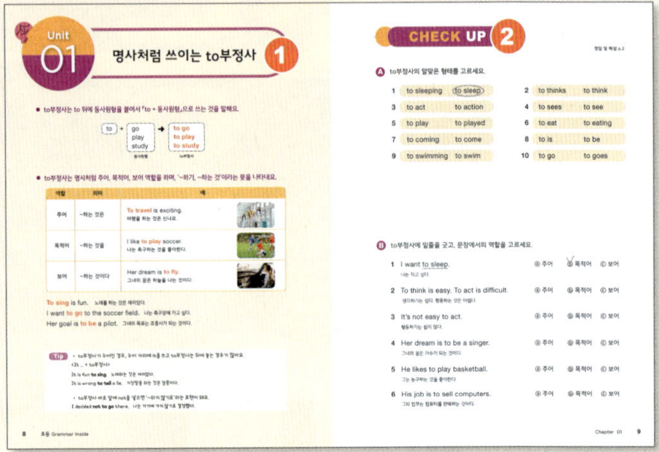

❶ 문법 설명

한눈에 들어오는 문법 설명과 예문으로 문법 개념을 쉽게 이해할 수 있어요.

❷ CHECK UP

간단한 확인 문제를 통해 문법 개념을 제대로 이해했는지 확인할 수 있어요.

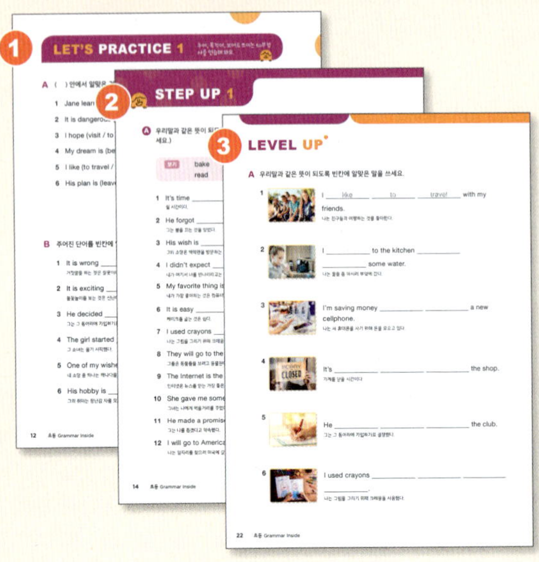

❶ LET'S PRACTICE

간단한 유형의 문제로 새로 학습한 내용을 충분히 이해했는지 점검할 수 있어요.

❷ STEP UP

빈칸 채우기부터 통문장 완성까지 다양한 유형의 문제를 풀어 보며 문법 포인트를 확실히 익힐 수 있어요.

❸ LEVEL UP

빈칸 채우기 활동으로 앞서 학습한 문장을 다시 써보고 문법 개념을 정확히 학습했는지 파악할 수 있어요.

실제 교내 평가 유형의 Chapter Review Test, 실전 Test, 총괄평가로 앞에서 배운 문법 내용을 복습해요.

본책에 쓰인 문장을 그대로 활용한 추가 문제를 풀어 보며 문법 개념을 제대로 익혔는지 확인해요.

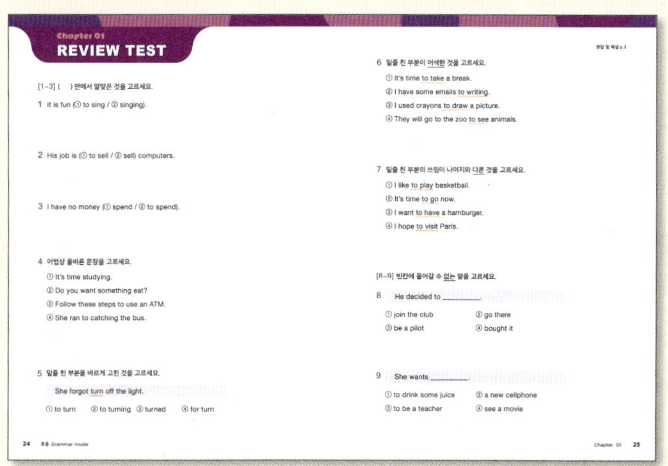

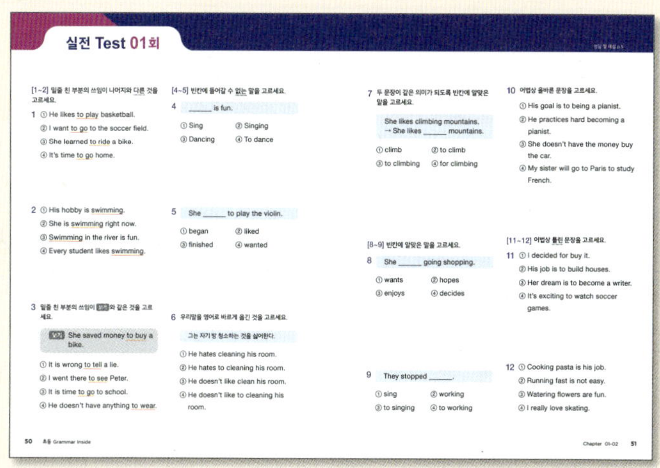

REVIEW TEST

다양한 유형의 객관식 문제와 서술형 문제를 통해 해당 챕터에서 배운 내용을 정리해볼 수 있어요.

실전 Test

두 개의 챕터를 학습 후에는 실제 교내 평가 유형의 문제를 통해 지금까지 배운 내용을 다시 상기할 수 있어요.

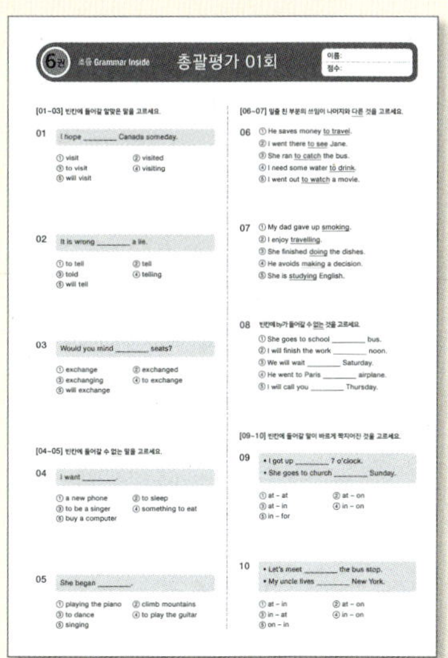

WORKBOOK

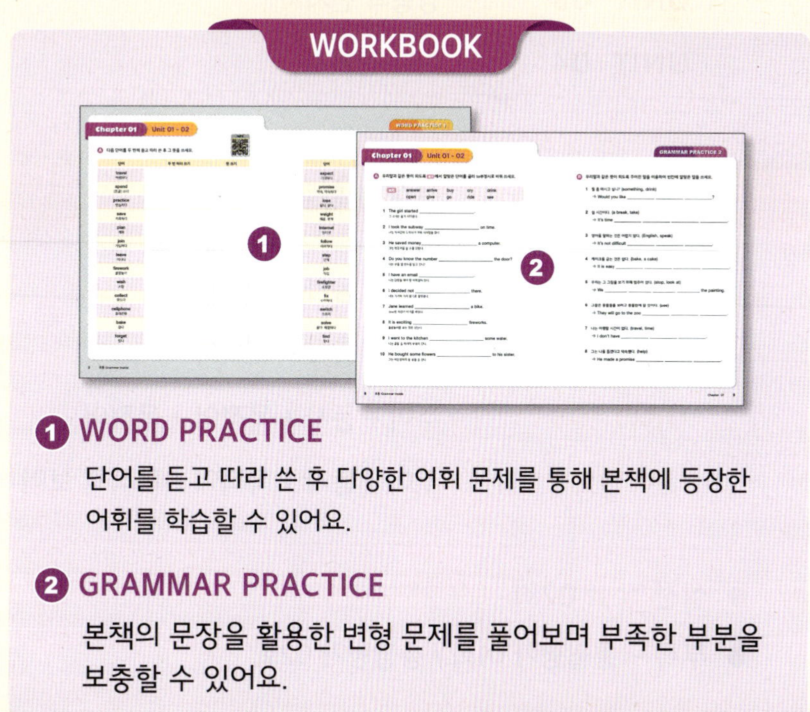

총괄평가

총 2회의 총괄평가를 통해 책 전체의 내용을 복습할 수 있어요.

❶ WORD PRACTICE

단어를 듣고 따라 쓴 후 다양한 어휘 문제를 통해 본책에 등장한 어휘를 학습할 수 있어요.

❷ GRAMMAR PRACTICE

본책의 문장을 활용한 변형 문제를 풀어보며 부족한 부분을 보충할 수 있어요.

목차

학습플랜

하루에 본책 두 개의 Unit을 학습하고 워크북으로 복습하는 구성입니다.
워크북을 수업에 활용 시 32차시 수업이 가능합니다.

차시	학습 내용		숙제	학습 날짜	
1 차시	CHAPTER 01 UNIT 01 - 02	CHECK UP LET'S PRACTICE 1~2	워크북 CH 01 UNIT 01~02	월	일
2 차시		STEP UP 1~4 LEVEL UP		월	일
3 차시	CHAPTER 01	REVIEW TEST		월	일
4 차시	CHAPTER 02 UNIT 01 - 02	CHECK UP LET'S PRACTICE 1~2	워크북 CH 02 UNIT 01~02	월	일
5 차시		STEP UP 1~4 LEVEL UP		월	일
6 차시	CHAPTER 02	REVIEW TEST		월	일
7 차시	실전 Test 01회			월	일
8 차시	CHAPTER 03 UNIT 01 - 02	CHECK UP LET'S PRACTICE 1~2	워크북 CH 03 UNIT 01~02	월	일
9 차시		STEP UP 1~4 LEVEL UP		월	일
10 차시	CHAPTER 03 UNIT 03 - 04	CHECK UP LET'S PRACTICE 1~2	워크북 CH 03 UNIT 03~04	월	일
11 차시		STEP UP 1~4 LEVEL UP		월	일
12 차시	CHAPTER 03	REVIEW TEST		월	일
13 차시	CHAPTER 04 UNIT 01 - 02	CHECK UP LET'S PRACTICE 1~2	워크북 CH 04 UNIT 01~02	월	일
14 차시		STEP UP 1~4 LEVEL UP		월	일
15 차시	CHAPTER 04 UNIT 03 - 04	CHECK UP LET'S PRACTICE 1~2	워크북 CH 04 UNIT 03~04	월	일
16 차시		STEP UP 1~4 LEVEL UP		월	일
17 차시	CHAPTER 04	REVIEW TEST		월	일
18 차시	실전 Test 02회			월	일
19 차시	총괄평가 01회			월	일
20 차시	총괄평가 02회			월	일

Chapter 01

to부정사

Unit 01 명사처럼 쓰이는 to부정사

Unit 02 형용사와 부사처럼 쓰이는 to부정사

학습목표

1 to부정사의 형태와 의미에 대해 알아보아요.
2 주어, 목적어, 보어 역할을 하는 to부정사에 대해 알아보아요.
3 명사를 꾸며주는 to부정사에 대해 알아보아요.
4 목적을 나타내는 to부정사에 대해 알아보아요.

WORD CHECK

travel
여행하다

job
일, 직업

spend
(돈을) 쓰다

practice
연습하다

save
저축하다

plan
계획

leave
떠나다

fireworks
불꽃놀이

join
가입하다

collect
모으다

cellphone
휴대전화

bake
굽다

forget
잊다

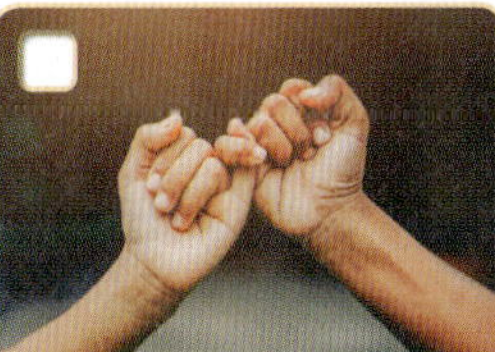

promise
약속, 약속하다

Internet
인터넷

weight
체중, 무게

fix
수리하다

firefighter
소방관

switch
스위치

solve
풀다, 해결하다

Unit 01 명사처럼 쓰이는 to부정사

● to부정사는 to 뒤에 동사원형을 붙여서 「to + 동사원형」으로 쓰는 것을 말해요.

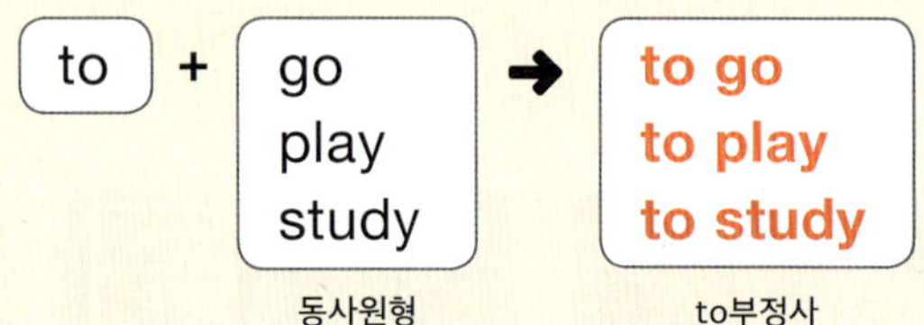

| to | + | go
play
study | ➡ | to go
to play
to study |

동사원형 　　　　　 to부정사

● to부정사는 명사처럼 주어, 목적어, 보어 역할을 하며, '~하기, ~하는 것'이라는 뜻을 나타내요.

역할	의미	예	
주어	~하는 것은	**To travel** is exciting. 여행을 하는 것은 신나요.	
목적어	~하는 것을	I like **to play** soccer. 나는 축구하는 것을 좋아한다.	
보어	~하는 것이다	Her dream is **to fly**. 그녀의 꿈은 하늘을 나는 것이다.	

To sing is fun. 　노래를 하는 것은 재미있다.

I want **to go** to the soccer field. 　나는 축구장에 가고 싶다.

Her goal is **to be** a pilot. 　그녀의 목표는 조종사가 되는 것이다.

> **Tip**　• to부정사가 주어인 경우, 주어 자리에 it을 쓰고 to부정사는 뒤에 놓는 경우가 많아요.
> <It ... + to부정사>
> It is fun **to sing**. 　노래를 하는 것은 재미있다.
> It is wrong **to tell** a lie. 　거짓말을 하는 것은 잘못이다.
>
> • to부정사 바로 앞에 not을 넣으면 '~하지 않기로'라는 표현이 돼요.
> I decided **not to go** there. 　나는 거기에 가지 않기로 결정했다.

CHECK UP

A to부정사의 알맞은 형태를 고르세요.

1	to sleeping (to sleep)	**2**	to thinks to think
3	to act to action	**4**	to sees to see
5	to play to played	**6**	to eat to eating
7	to coming to come	**8**	to is to be
9	to swimming to swim	**10**	to go to goes

B to부정사에 밑줄을 긋고, 문장에서의 역할을 고르세요.

1 I want to sleep.   ⓐ 주어   ⓑ 목적어   ⓒ 보어
나는 자고 싶다.

2 To think is easy. To act is difficult.   ⓐ 주어   ⓑ 목적어   ⓒ 보어
생각하기는 쉽다. 행동하는 것은 어렵다.

3 It's not easy to act.   ⓐ 주어   ⓑ 목적어   ⓒ 보어
행동하기는 쉽지 않다.

4 Her dream is to be a singer.   ⓐ 주어   ⓑ 목적어   ⓒ 보어
그녀의 꿈은 가수가 되는 것이다.

5 He likes to play basketball.   ⓐ 주어   ⓑ 목적어   ⓒ 보어
그는 농구하는 것을 좋아한다.

6 His job is to sell computers.   ⓐ 주어   ⓑ 목적어   ⓒ 보어
그의 일은 컴퓨터를 판매하는 것이다.

Unit 02

형용사와 부사처럼 쓰이는 to부정사

● to부정사는 형용사처럼 명사나 대명사를 꾸며줄 수 있어요. 이때 to부정사는 꾸밈을 받는 명사나 대명사의 뒤에 놓이며, '~할, ~해야 할'이라는 뜻이에요.

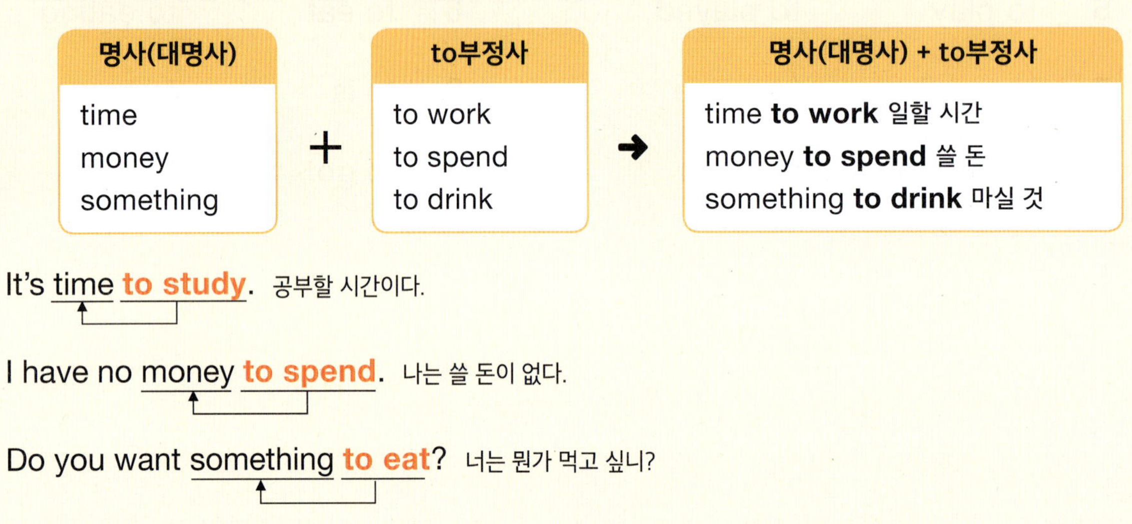

명사(대명사)		to부정사		명사(대명사) + to부정사
time money something	+	to work to spend to drink	→	time **to work** 일할 시간 money **to spend** 쓸 돈 something **to drink** 마실 것

It's time **to study**. 공부할 시간이다.

I have no money **to spend**. 나는 쓸 돈이 없다.

Do you want something **to eat**? 너는 뭔가 먹고 싶니?

● 부사처럼 쓰이는 to부정사는 '~하기 위해, ~하려고'라는 뜻으로 목적을 나타낼 수 있어요.

Tom practices hard. Tom은 열심히 연습한다.	+	He will become a soccer player. 그는 축구 선수가 될 것이다.

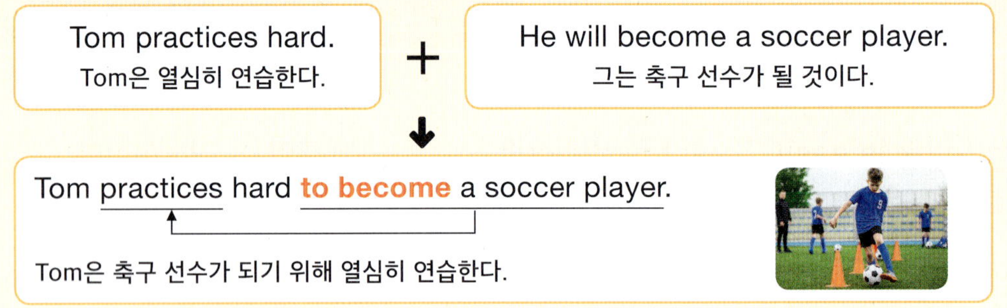

Tom practices hard **to become** a soccer player.

Tom은 축구 선수가 되기 위해 열심히 연습한다.

He saves money **to travel**. 그는 여행을 하기 위해 돈을 모은다.

I went there **to see** Jane. 나는 Jane을 보기 위해 거기에 갔다.

> **Tip** 문장 안에서 to부정사 역할을 비교해 봐요.
>
> I like **to play** baseball. 나는 야구를 하는 것을 좋아한다. (명사 역할)
> 　　　목적어
>
> I found a good place **to play** baseball. 나는 야구하기에 좋은 장소를 찾았다. (형용사 역할)
> 　　　앞의 명사를 꾸며줌
>
> I went there **to play** baseball with my friends. 나는 친구들과 야구를 하기 위해 거기에 갔다. (부사 역할)
> 　　　앞의 동사를 꾸며줌

CHECK UP

A 밑줄 친 to부정사의 뜻으로 알맞은 것을 [보기]에서 고르세요.

[보기]　　ⓐ ~할　　　　ⓑ ~하기 위해, ~하려고

1 She ran <u>to catch</u> the bus.　　　　ⓑ

2 I don't have anything <u>to wear</u>.

3 I have a friend <u>to call</u>.

4 He will go to Australia <u>to look</u> for work.

5 Do you know the number <u>to open</u> the door?

B 사진을 보고 알맞은 말에 V 표시하세요.

1 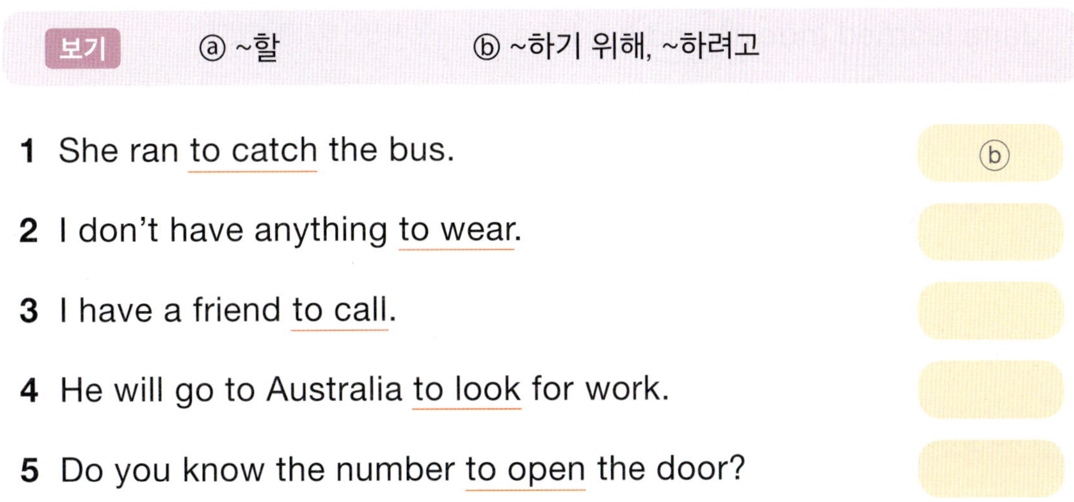

She gave me a book ☑ to read / ☐ read .

그녀는 나에게 읽을 책을 주었다.

2

I need some water ☐ to drink / ☐ drinking .

나는 마실 물이 좀 필요하다.

3

I went out ☐ to watch / ☐ watched a movie.

나는 영화를 보러 나갔다.

4 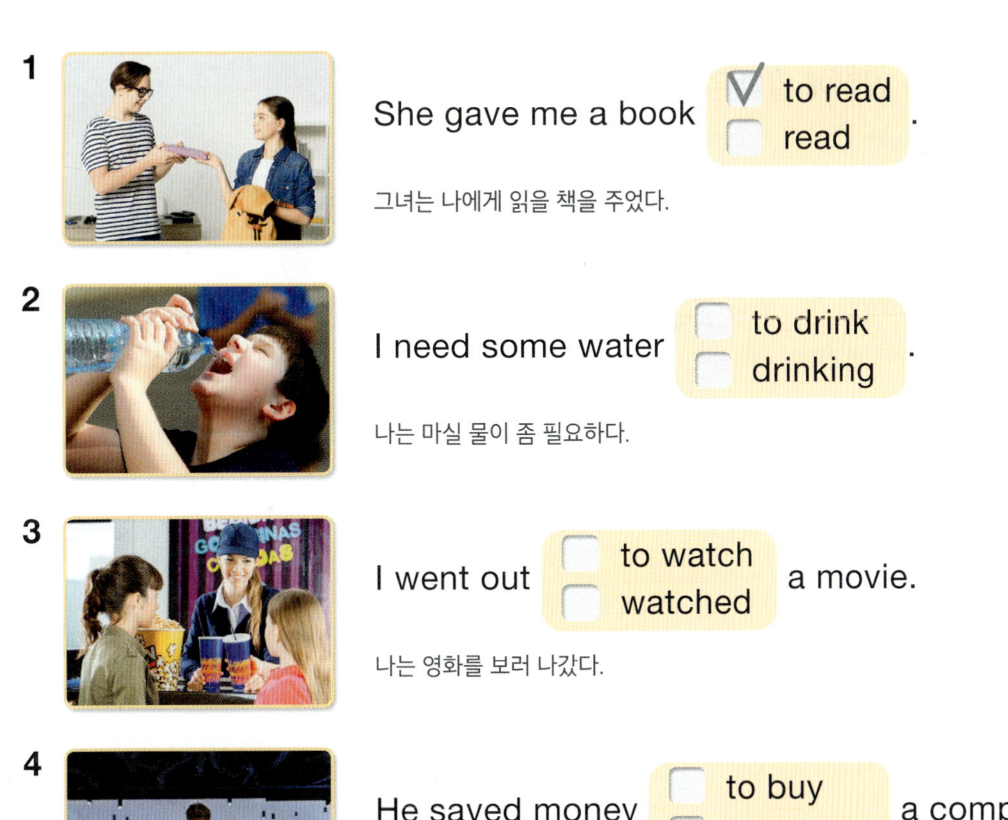

He saved money ☐ to buy / ☐ to buying a computer.

그는 컴퓨터를 살 돈을 모았다.

A (   ) 안에서 알맞은 것을 고르세요.

1 Jane learned (ride / to ride) a bike.   Jane은 자전거 타기를 배웠다.

2 It is dangerous (swim / to swim) in the river.   강에서 수영하는 것은 위험하다.

3 I hope (visit / to visit) New York someday.   나는 언젠가 뉴욕을 방문하고 싶다.

4 My dream is (become / to become) a great writer.   내 꿈은 훌륭한 작가가 되는 것이다.

5 I like (to travel / travel) with my friends.   나는 친구들과 여행하는 것을 좋아한다.

6 His plan is (leave / to leave) early.   그의 계획은 일찍 떠나는 것이다.

B 주어진 단어를 빈칸에 알맞은 형태로 쓰세요.

1 It is wrong _______ to _______ _______ tell _______ a lie. (tell)
거짓말을 하는 것은 잘못이다.

2 It is exciting _______________ _______________ fireworks. (see)
불꽃놀이를 보는 것은 신난다.

3 He decided _______________ _______________ the club. (join)
그는 그 동아리에 가입하기로 결정했다.

4 The girl started _______________ _______________. (cry)
그 소녀는 울기 시작했다.

5 One of my wishes is _______________ _______________ Canada. (visit)
내 소망 중 하나는 캐나다를 방문하는 것이다.

6 His hobby is _______________ _______________ toy cars. (collect)
그의 취미는 장난감 차를 모으는 것이다.

LET'S PRACTICE 2

형용사와 부사처럼 쓰이는 to부정사를 연습해 봐요.

정답 및 해설 p.2

A 우리말과 같은 뜻이 되도록 보기 에서 알맞은 단어를 골라 to부정사로 바꾸세요.

보기	do	drink	get	play	sell	spend	study

1 공부할 시간 ➡ time _____to study_____

2 쓸 돈 ➡ money ___________________

3 마실 것 ➡ something ___________________

4 할 일 ➡ work ___________________

5 팔려는 책 ➡ a book ___________________

6 놀 시간 ➡ time ___________________

B 밑줄 친 부분을 바르게 고쳐 쓰세요.

1 I took the subway <u>arrive</u> on time. ➡ _____to arrive_____
나는 제시간에 도착하기 위해 지하철을 탔다.

2 He bought some flowers <u>giving</u> to his sister. ➡ ___________________
그는 여동생에게 줄 꽃을 좀 샀다.

3 This is the best time <u>start</u>. ➡ ___________________
지금이 시작하기에 가장 좋은 시간이다.

4 I went to the kitchen <u>drink</u> some water. ➡ ___________________
나는 물을 좀 마시러 부엌에 갔다.

5 I'm saving money <u>buying</u> a new cellphone. ➡ ___________________
나는 새 휴대폰을 사기 위해 돈을 모으고 있다.

6 She will go to New York <u>study</u> English. ➡ ___________________
그녀는 영어를 공부하기 위해 뉴욕에 갈 것이다.

A 우리말과 같은 뜻이 되도록 [보기]에서 알맞은 말을 골라 쓰세요. (필요하면 형태를 바꾸세요.)

보기	bake	draw	get	help	look for	play
	read	see	take	turn off	visit	meet

1 It's time _______________ to take _______________ a break.
쉴 시간이다.

2 He forgot _______________________ the light.
그는 불을 끄는 것을 잊었다.

3 His wish is _______________________ the White House.
그의 소망은 백악관을 방문하는 것이다.

4 I didn't expect _______________________ you here.
내가 여기서 너를 만나리라고는 생각하지 못했다.

5 My favorite thing is _______________________ computer games.
내가 가장 좋아하는 것은 컴퓨터 게임을 하는 것이다.

6 It is easy _______________________ a cake.
케이크를 굽는 것은 쉽다.

7 I used crayons _______________________ a picture.
나는 그림을 그리기 위해 크레용을 사용했다.

8 They will go to the zoo _______________________ animals.
그들은 동물들을 보려고 동물원에 갈 것이다.

9 The Internet is the best way _______________________ the news.
인터넷은 뉴스를 얻는 가장 좋은 방법이다.

10 She gave me something _______________________.
그녀는 나에게 먹을거리를 주었다.

11 He made a promise _______________________ me.
그는 나를 돕겠다고 약속했다.

12 I will go to America _______________________ work.
나는 일자리를 찾으려 미국에 갈 것이다.

B 밑줄 친 부분을 to부정사를 사용하여 바르게 고쳐 쓰세요.

1 I don't have time <u>travel</u>.
나는 여행할 시간이 없다.
→ _____to travel_____

2 I hate <u>lose</u>.
나는 지는 것을 싫어한다.
→ ____________

3 It's not difficult <u>speaking</u> English.
영어를 말하는 것은 어렵지 않다.
→ ____________

4 I studied hard <u>getting</u> a good mark.
나는 좋은 점수를 얻기 위해 열심히 공부했다.
→ ____________

5 Would you like something <u>drink</u>?
뭘 좀 마시고 싶니?
→ ____________

6 His plan is <u>buy</u> a new computer.
그의 계획은 새 컴퓨터를 사는 것이다.
→ ____________

7 Do you want <u>buying</u> a new smartphone?
너는 새 스마트폰을 사고 싶니?
→ ____________

8 I don't have anything <u>wearing</u>.
나는 입을 것이 없다.
→ ____________

9 We stopped <u>look</u> at the painting.
우리는 그 그림을 보기 위해 멈추어 섰다.
→ ____________

10 I have some emails <u>written</u>.
나는 써야 할 이메일들이 좀 있다.
→ ____________

11 I got up early <u>doing</u> my homework.
나는 숙제를 하기 위해 일찍 일어났다.
→ ____________

12 I started <u>read</u> the novel yesterday.
나는 그 소설을 어제 읽기 시작했다.
→ ____________

A 주어진 말을 이용하여 빈칸에 알맞은 말을 쓰세요.

1 I ___like___ ___to___ ___play___ baseball. (like, play)
나는 야구하는 것을 좋아한다.

2 I ___________ ___________ ___________ to the park. (want, go)
나는 공원에 가고 싶다.

3 His dream ___________ ___________ ___________ the world. (is, travel)　그의 꿈은 세계를 여행하는 것이다.

4 His goal ___________ ___________ ___________ weight. (is, lose)
그의 목표는 몸무게를 줄이는 것이다.

5 It is ___________ ___________ ___________ in the sea. (fun, swim)
바다에서 수영하는 것은 재미있다.

6 It is ___________ ___________ ___________ animals. (wrong, hurt)
동물을 해치는 것은 잘못이다.

7 It's ___________ ___________ ___________ the shop. (time, close)
가게를 닫을 시간이다.

8 I have no ___________ ___________ ___________ a new phone.
(money, buy)　새 전화기를 살 돈이 없다.

9 I want ___________ ___________ ___________. (something, read)
나는 읽을 것을 원한다.

10 She practices ___________ ___________ ___________ English
well. (hard, speak)　그녀는 영어를 잘하기 위해 열심히 연습한다.

11 I went ___________ ___________ ___________ my computer. (there, fix)　나는 내 컴퓨터를 고치기 위해 거기에 갔다.

12 She ran ___________ ___________ ___________ her book. (home, get)　그녀는 자신의 책을 가지러 집으로 달려갔다.

B 사진을 보고 주어진 말을 이용하여 빈칸에 알맞은 말을 쓰세요.

1

A: Where do you want to go?
너는 어디를 가고 싶니?

B: I want ____to____ ____go____ to the mountains.
(go)   나는 산에 가고 싶어.

2

A: What's her dream?
그녀의 꿈은 뭐니?

B: Her dream is ____________ ____________ Paris. (visit)
그녀의 꿈은 파리를 방문하는 거야.

3

A: Do you like drawing?
너는 그림 그리기를 좋아하니?

B: Yes. It is fun ____________ ____________ pets. (draw)
응. 애완동물을 그리는 것은 재미있어.

4

A: I have something ____________ ____________ you.
(give)   나는 너에게 줄 게 있어.

B: What is it?
뭔데?

5

A: Why did you go there?
너는 왜 거기에 갔니?

B: I went there ____________ ____________ soccer with
my friends. (play)   나는 친구들과 축구를 하려고 거기에 갔어.

6

A: What is Tom doing?
Tom은 무엇을 하고 있니?

B: He is studying hard ____________ ____________ the
test. (pass)   그는 시험에 합격하기 위해 열심히 공부하고 있어.

A 우리말과 같은 뜻이 되도록 주어진 말을 바르게 배열하세요.

1 나는 너에게 할 말이 있다. (to / tell / something)

→ I have _______ something to tell _______ you.

2 그는 토요일에 나를 방문하기로 약속했다. (visit / to / a promise)

→ He made _______________________________ me on Saturday.

3 나는 쓸 돈이 좀 있다. (spend / to / some money)

→ I have _______________________________.

4 앱을 다운 받으려면 이 단계들을 따르세요. (download / to / the apps)

→ Follow these steps _______________________________.

5 나는 친구와 점심을 먹으려고 나갔다. (lunch / have / to)

→ I went out _______________________________ with my friend.

6 그는 세계를 여행하기 위해 돈을 모은다. (the world / travel / to)

→ He saves money _______________________________.

7 그는 열일곱 살에 운전을 배웠다. (to / learned / drive)

→ He _______________________________ when he was 17.

8 그 게임을 보는 것은 무척 신난다. (to / the games / see)

→ It is exciting _______________________________.

9 그의 희망은 가수가 되는 것이다. (a singer / be / to)

→ His hope is _______________________________.

10 그녀의 일은 영어를 가르치는 것이다. (teach / to / English)

→ Her job is _______________________________.

B 우리말과 같은 뜻이 되도록 보기 의 단어를 이용하여 문장을 완성하세요.

보기   drive   arrive   become   buy   do   get   say   visit

1 비가 내리는데 운전하는 것은 위험하다.

→ It is dangerous _______________ to drive _______________ in the rain.

2 내 꿈은 소방관이 되는 것이다.

→ My dream is _______________________ a firefighter.

3 나는 언젠가 Canada를 방문하고 싶다.

→ I hope _______________________ Canada someday.

4 나는 제시간에 도착하려고 택시를 탔다.

→ I took a taxi _______________________ on time.

5 지금이 그것을 하기에 가장 적절한 때이다.

→ This is the best time _______________________ that.

6 나는 소금을 좀 가지러 부엌에 갔다.

→ I went to the kitchen _______________________ some salt.

7 나는 새 자전거를 사기 위해 돈을 저축하고 있다.

→ I'm saving money _______________________ a new bike.

8 나는 너한테 할 말이 없다.

→ I don't have anything _______________________ to you.

STEP UP 4

A 우리말과 같은 뜻이 되도록 주어진 말을 이용하여 문장을 완성하세요.

1 동물을 해치는 것은 잘못이다. (it, wrong, animals, hurt)

→ _It is wrong to hurt animals._

2 집에 갈 시간이다. (it, time, go, home)

→ ____

3 그는 스위치를 끄는 것을 잊었다. (forgot, the switch, turn off)

→ ____

4 우리는 서로 만나리라고 기대하지 않았다. (didn't, expect, each other, see)

→ ____

5 내가 가장 좋아하는 것은 음악을 듣는 것이다. (favorite thing, listen to, music)

→ ____

6 그 문제를 푸는 것은 쉽다. (it, easy, the problem, solve)

→ ____

7 나는 그림을 그리기 위해 연필을 샀다. (bought, a pencil, a picture, draw)

→ ____

8 그의 소망은 청와대를 방문하는 것이다. (wish, the Blue House, visit)

→ ____

9 나는 먹을 게 필요하다. (need, eat, something)

→ ____

10 그는 더 나아지기 위해 열심히 연습한다. (practices, hard, better, become)

→ ____

B (   ) 안의 말을 알맞은 곳에 넣어 문장을 완성하세요.

1 He ran the train. (to catch)   그는 기차를 타려고 달렸다.

➡ He ran to catch the train.

2 Her dream is a writer. (to be)   그녀의 꿈은 작가가 되는 것이다.

➡ ______________________________________

3 His job is books. (to sell)   그의 일은 책을 파는 것이다.

➡ ______________________________________

4 I found a good place. (to study)   나는 공부하기에 좋은 장소를 발견했다.

➡ ______________________________________

5 He likes tennis. (to play)   그는 테니스 치는 것을 좋아한다.

➡ ______________________________________

6 We have no time. (to waste)   우리는 낭비할 시간이 없다.

➡ ______________________________________

7 He is saving money to London. (to go)   그는 런던에 가려고 돈을 모으고 있다.

➡ ______________________________________

8 I went there soccer. (to play)   나는 거기에 축구하러 갔다.

➡ ______________________________________

9 I have a friend me. (to help)   나는 나를 도와줄 친구가 있다.

➡ ______________________________________

10 I need time my email. (to check)   나는 내 이메일을 확인할 시간이 필요하다.

➡ ______________________________________

LEVEL UP

A 우리말과 같은 뜻이 되도록 빈칸에 알맞은 말을 쓰세요.

1   I _____like_____ _____to_____ _____travel_____ with my friends.

나는 친구들과 여행하는 것을 좋아한다.

2   I _____________ to the kitchen _____________ _____________ some water.

나는 물을 좀 마시러 부엌에 갔다.

3   I'm saving money _____________ _____________ a new cellphone.

나는 새 휴대폰을 사기 위해 돈을 모으고 있다.

4   It's _____________ _____________ _____________ the shop.

가게를 닫을 시간이다.

5   He _____________ _____________ _____________ the club.

그는 그 동아리에 가입하기로 결정했다.

6   I used crayons _____________ _____________ _____________ _____________.

나는 그림을 그리기 위해 크레용을 사용했다.

B 우리말과 같은 뜻이 되도록 빈칸에 알맞은 말을 쓰세요.

1 I don't have ___________ time ___________ to ___________ travel ___________.
나는 여행할 시간이 없다.

2 ___________ ___________ dangerous ___________
___________ in the river. 강에서 수영하는 것은 위험하다.

3 He forgot ___________ ___________ ___________ the light.
그는 불을 끄는 것을 잊었다.

4 This is the best ___________ ___________ ___________.
지금이 시작하기에 가장 좋은 시간이다.

5 He likes ___________ ___________ ___________.
그는 농구하는 것을 좋아한다.

6 I don't have ___________ ___________ ___________.
나는 입을 게 전혀 없다.

7 Do you know the number ___________ ___________
___________ ___________ ? 너는 그 문을 열 수 있는 번호를 아니?

8 Jane ___________ ___________ ___________ a bike.
Jane은 자전거 타기를 배웠다.

9 I took the subway ___________ ___________ on time.
나는 제시간에 도착하기 위해 지하철을 탔다.

10 His plan is ___________ ___________ ___________.
그의 계획은 일찍 떠나는 것이다.

11 The girl ___________ ___________ ___________.
그 소녀는 울기 시작했다.

12 We ___________ ___________ ___________ at the painting.
우리는 그 그림을 보기 위해 멈추어 섰다.

[1~3] (   ) 안에서 알맞은 것을 고르세요.

1 It is fun (① to sing / ② singing).

2 His job is (① to sell / ② sell) computers.

3 I have no money (① spend / ② to spend).

4 어법상 올바른 문장을 고르세요.

① It's time studying.

② Do you want something eat?

③ Follow these steps to use an ATM.

④ She ran to catching the bus.

5 밑줄 친 부분을 바르게 고친 것을 고르세요.

She forgot <u>turn</u> off the light.

① to turn   ② to turning   ③ turned   ④ for turn

6 밑줄 친 부분이 <u>어색한</u> 것을 고르세요.

① It's time to take a break.

② I have some emails to writing.

③ I used crayons to draw a picture.

④ They will go to the zoo to see animals.

7 밑줄 친 부분의 쓰임이 나머지와 <u>다른</u> 것을 고르세요.

① I like to play basketball.

② It's time to go now.

③ I want to have a hamburger.

④ I hope to visit Paris.

[8~9] 빈칸에 들어갈 수 <u>없는</u> 말을 고르세요.

8 He decided to ____________.

① join the club ② go there

③ be a pilot ④ bought it

9 She wants ____________.

① to drink some juice ② a new cellphone

③ to be a teacher ④ see a movie

10 빈칸에 공통으로 알맞은 말을 고르세요.

> · The Internet is the best way __________ the news.
> · I studied hard __________ a good mark.

① to get ② get ③ getting ④ to getting

11 빈칸에 들어갈 말이 바르게 짝지어진 것을 고르세요.

> · It is wrong __________ animals.
> · I went there __________ animals.

① hurting – seeing ② to hurt – to see

③ hurting – to see ④ to hurt – saw

12 밑줄 친 부분이 올바른 것을 고르세요.

① His goal is to losing weight.

② I want something to reading.

③ I went there fixed my computer.

④ We stopped to look at the painting.

13 우리말을 영어로 바르게 옮긴 것을 고르세요.

> 나는 써야 할 이메일들이 좀 있다.

① I have some emails to writing.

② I have some emails to write.

③ I have some emails write.

④ I have some emails writing.

14 어법상 <u>틀린</u> 부분을 찾아 바르게 고쳐 쓰세요.

> Follow these steps to downloading the apps.

______________________ ➡ ______________________

15 주어진 단어를 빈칸에 알맞은 형태로 쓰세요.

> A: Where do you want (1) __________? (go)
> B: Let's go to the restaurant. I want something (2) __________. (eat)

(1) ______________________   (2) ______________________

16 그림을 보고 주어진 말을 이용하여 빈칸에 알맞은 말을 쓰세요.

I love __________ __________ baseball. (play) I want __________ __________ an excellent baseball player. (be) My dream is __________ __________ an MLB player. (become) So I'm going __________ __________ __________ __________ and hit the ball. (learn, catch) By the way, do you know the way __________ __________ a home run? (hit)

Chapter 02

동명사

Unit 01 동명사의 형태와 역할

Unit 02 목적어로 쓰이는 동명사와 to부정사

1 동명사의 형태와 의미에 대해 알아보아요.
2 주어, 목적어, 보어 역할을 하는 동명사에 대해 알아보아요.
3 동명사를 목적어로 취하는 동사에 대해 알아보아요.
4 to부정사를 목적어로 취하는 동사에 대해 알아보아요.

WORD CHECK

cycle
자전거를 타다

ski
스키

snowman
눈사람

clean
청소하다

exercise
운동하다

quit
그만두다

exchange
교환하다

fishing
낚시

grow
기르다

prize
상, 상품

forest
숲

asleep
잠이 든

bathroom
화장실

jog
조깅하다

shout
소리치다

volume
음량

headache
두통

explain
설명하다

sandwich
샌드위치

mistake
실수

동명사의 형태와 역할

● 동명사는 동사원형에 -ing를 붙여 명사처럼 쓰는 말이에요. '~하는 것', '~하기'라는 뜻이에요.
동명사를 만드는 방법은 현재진행형에서 '동사원형-ing'를 만드는 방법과 같아요.

● 동명사는 명사처럼 주어, 목적어, 보어 역할을 할 수 있어요.

역할	쓰임	예
주어	동명사는 문장 맨 앞의 주어 자리에 쓸 수 있어요. 이때 동명사는 3인칭 단수 취급해요.	Cycling is exciting. 자전거 타기는 신난다.
목적어	동명사는 일반동사 뒤에 쓸 수 있어요.	I enjoy skiing. 나는 스키 타는 것을 즐긴다.
보어	동명사는 be동사 뒤에 쓸 수 있어요.	Her hobby is watching YouTube. 그녀의 취미는 유튜브를 보는 것이다.

Dancing is fun. 춤추는 것은 재미있다.
Making a snowman is not difficult. 눈사람을 만드는 것은 어렵지 않다.
I hate cycling. 나는 자전거 타기를 싫어한다.
My hobby is cycling. 내 취미는 자전거 타기이다.

Tip
• 동명사는 자신의 목적어를 가질 수도 있어요. (동명사 + 동명사의 목적어)
Making cakes is fun. 케이크를 만드는 것은 재미있다.
Cleaning your room is boring. 네 방을 청소하는 것은 지루하다.
His hobby is watching YouTube. 그의 취미는 유튜브를 보는 것이다.

• '동사원형-ing' 형태가 be동사 뒤에 쓰일 때 '~하는 것'으로 해석되면 동명사, '~하는 중이다'로 해석되면 현재진행형이에요.
His hobby is playing tennis. 그의 취미는 테니스를 치는 것이다. (~하는 것: 동명사)
He is playing tennis right now. 그는 지금 테니스를 치는 중이다. (~하는 중이다: 현재진행형)

CHECK UP

A 동명사의 알맞은 형태를 고르세요.

1 comeing (coming) **2** rideing riding

3 swiming swimming **4** believing believeing

5 dancing danceing **6** eatting eating

7 takeing taking **8** listenning listening

9 beginning begining **10** wining winning

B 동명사에 밑줄을 긋고 문장에서의 역할을 고르세요.

1 She enjoys <u>running</u> daily. ⓐ 주어 ⓑ 목적어 ⓒ 보어
그녀는 매일 달리기 하는 것을 즐긴다.

2 Swimming is his hobby. ⓐ 주어 ⓑ 목적어 ⓒ 보어
수영이 그의 취미이다.

3 Exercising is good for your body. ⓐ 주어 ⓑ 목적어 ⓒ 보어
운동은 몸에 좋다.

4 What Jane really loves is skiing. ⓐ 주어 ⓑ 목적어 ⓒ 보어
Jane이 정말로 좋아하는 것은 스키 타기이다.

5 I finished doing my homework. ⓐ 주어 ⓑ 목적어 ⓒ 보어
나는 내 숙제를 끝마쳤다.

6 My cat's favorite activity is jumping. ⓐ 주어 ⓑ 목적어 ⓒ 보어
내 고양이가 가장 좋아하는 활동은 뛰어오르기이다.

목적어로 쓰이는 동명사와 to부정사

- 뒤에 목적어가 필요한 일반동사 중에는 목적어로 동명사를 쓰는 동사와 to부정사를 쓰는 동사가 있어요.

동명사를 목적어로 취하는 동사			
enjoy 즐기다	keep 계속하다	finish 끝내다	give up 포기하다
stop 중단하다	quit 그만두다	avoid 피하다	mind 꺼리다, 싫어하다

I **enjoy travelling**. 나는 여행을 즐긴다.

She **finished doing** the dishes. 그녀는 설거지를 끝냈다.

Dad **gave up smoking**. 아빠는 담배를 끊으셨다.

He **avoids making** a decision. 그는 결정을 내리는 것을 피한다.

Would you **mind exchanging** seats? 자리를 바꿀 수 있을까요?

to부정사를 목적어로 취하는 동사			
want 원하다	hope 희망하다	wish 바라다	plan 계획하다
need 필요하다	choose 고르다	decide 결심하다	promise 약속하다

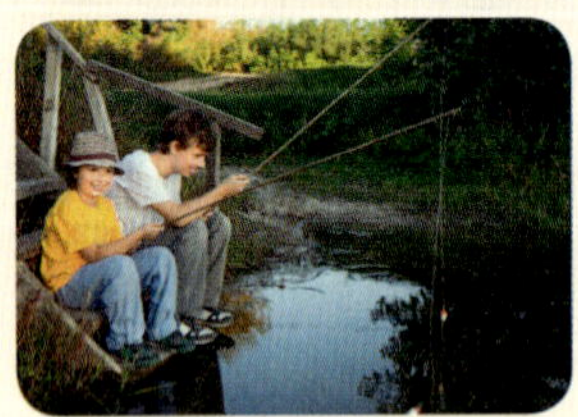

I **plan to go** fishing. 나는 낚시하러 갈 계획이다.

I **want to be** alone. 나는 혼자 있고 싶다.

They **hope to succeed**. 그들은 성공하기를 희망한다.

Mr. Jones **wishes to see** you. Jones씨가 당신을 보기를 원한다.

She **decided to grow** her hair. 그녀는 머리를 기르기로 결정했다.

- 다음 동사들은 동명사와 to부정사 모두를 목적어로 쓸 수 있어요.

begin 시작하다   start 시작하다   like 좋아하다   love 사랑하다   hate 싫어하다

She **began playing[to play]** the piano when she was five.
그녀는 다섯 살 때 피아노를 치기 시작했다.

I **like climbing[to climb]** mountains. 나는 등산을 좋아한다.

정답 및 해설 p.3

A 밑줄 친 목적어의 형태가 올바르면 ○, 올바르지 않으면 X 표시하세요.

1 enjoy shopping   ○   **2** want being a teacher

3 stop working   **4** decide to sell

5 like cooking   **6** promise helping me

7 finish to eating   **8** start talking

9 hope getting it   **10** plan to go

B 사진을 보고 알맞은 말에 V 표시하세요.

1 He began ☑ playing / ☐ play the guitar.

그는 기타 연주를 시작했다.

2 They started ☐ to dance / ☐ dance.

그들은 춤을 추기 시작했다.

3 I hate ☐ to waiting / ☐ waiting for the bus.

나는 버스를 기다리는 게 싫다.

4 I love ☐ winning / ☐ to winning prizes.

나는 상을 받는 게 너무 좋다.

A 빈칸에 들어갈 말로 알맞은 것을 고르세요.

1 __________ a bike is exciting. ⓐ Ride ⓑ Riding ✓
자전거 타기는 신난다.

2 He enjoys __________ birds. ⓐ to watch ⓑ watching
그는 새 관찰을 즐긴다.

3 One of the best hobbies is __________. ⓐ swimming ⓑ swim
가장 좋은 취미 중 하나는 수영이다.

4 __________ is good for your health. ⓐ Running ⓑ Run
달리기는 건강에 좋다.

5 He hates __________ up early. ⓐ wake ⓑ waking
그는 일찍 일어나는 것을 싫어한다.

6 One of my duties is __________ homework. ⓐ do ⓑ doing
내 의무 중 하나는 숙제를 하는 것이다.

B 밑줄 친 부분을 바르게 고쳐 한 단어로 쓰세요.

1 Write in English is difficult. → __Writing__
영어로 쓰는 것은 어렵다.

2 She doesn't like cook. → __________
그녀는 요리하는 것을 좋아하지 않는다.

3 What Tom really loves is paint pictures. → __________
Tom이 정말 좋아하는 것은 그림 그리기이다.

4 Read a book is interesting. → __________
책 읽기는 재미있다.

5 Do you enjoy to walking in the forest? → __________
너는 숲속에서 걷는 걸 좋아하니?

정답 및 해설 p.4

A ( ) 안에서 알맞은 것을 고르세요.

1 He can keep (run / running) for an hour.
그는 한 시간 동안 달리기를 할 수 있다.

2 The baby stopped (cry / crying) and fell asleep.
그 아기는 울기를 멈추고 잠들었다.

3 He avoids (to meet / meeting) her.
그는 그녀를 만나기를 꺼린다.

4 Katie chose (to stay / staying) away from work that day.
Katie는 그날 일하지 않기로 했다.

5 I wish (to visit / visiting) you in the summer, if possible.
여름에 당신을 방문하고 싶어요, 가능하다면.

B 밑줄 친 부분이 맞으면 ○, 틀리면 X 표시하세요.

1 I hate washing the dishes. → ○
나는 설거지 하는 것을 싫어한다.

2 My dad quit to smoke. →
아빠는 담배를 끊으셨다.

3 I need to go to the bathroom. →
나는 화장실에 가야 해.

4 They hope to visit us next year. →
그들은 내년에 우리를 방문하길 원한다.

5 He gave up to jog a few years ago. →
그는 몇 년 전에 조깅을 그만 두었다.

6 He promised calling me every week. →
그는 내게 매주 전화하겠다고 약속했다.

A 주어진 단어를 동명사로 바꾸어 빈칸에 쓰세요.

1 All my family enjoy ______skiing______. (ski)
우리 가족은 모두 스키 타기를 즐긴다.

2 __________________ is a cheap way to get around. (cycle)
자전거 타기는 돈을 적게 들이고 돌아다닐 수 있는 방법이다.

3 Many people love __________________ in the country. (live)
많은 사람들이 시골에 사는 것을 무척 좋아한다.

4 Is __________________ a cheap computer really a good idea? (buy)
싼 컴퓨터를 사는 것이 정말 좋은 생각인가요?

5 I go __________________ twice a week. (swim)
나는 일주일에 두 번 수영하러 간다.

6 Stop __________________ with your food! (play)
음식 가지고 장난 그만 해!

7 __________________ is an important part of the job. (listen)
듣기는 그 일의 중요한 부분이다.

8 I hate __________________ exams. (take)
나는 시험 치는 게 싫다.

9 I don't mind __________________. (wait)
나는 기다려도 괜찮다.

10 __________________ is the best form of learning. (teach)
가르치는 일은 배움의 가장 좋은 형태이다

11 For him, __________________ friends is a simple thing to do. (make)
그에게는 친구를 사귀는 일이 하기 쉬운 것이다.

12 Would you mind __________________ the window, please? (open)
창문을 열어도 될까요?

B 우리말과 같은 뜻이 되도록 보기 에서 알맞은 말을 골라 쓰세요.

보기					
turning	going	reading	meeting	shouting	trying
to eat	to feel	to leave	to lose	to stay	

1 Do you mind ______turning______ down the volume a little?
볼륨을 약간 줄여 줄래요?

2 Most people need ________________ loved.
대부분의 사람들은 사랑받는다고 느끼는 것이 필요하다

3 I enjoy ________________ people and seeing new places.
나는 사람들을 만나고 새로운 곳을 보는 것을 즐긴다.

4 He keeps ________________ to win games.
그는 게임을 이기려고 계속 노력한다.

5 Did you finish ________________ that magazine?
너는 그 잡지를 다 읽었니?

6 Stop ________________! You're giving me a headache!
소리 지르지 마! 너 때문에 내가 골치가 아파!

7 What do you want ________________?
너는 무엇을 먹고 싶니?

8 I'm not planning ________________ here for long.
나는 여기에 오래 머무를 계획이 없다.

9 He needs ________________ some weight.
그는 몸무게를 줄일 필요가 있다.

10 I was hoping ________________ here early today.
나는 오늘 일찍 여길 떠나길 바라고 있었다.

11 I try to avoid ________________ shopping on Saturdays.
나는 토요일에 쇼핑하러 가는 것을 피하려고 한다.

A 우리말과 같은 뜻이 되도록 보기 에서 알맞은 말을 골라 쓰세요. (필요하면 형태를 바꾸세요.)

> 보기　do　　explain　talk　write　work　cycle
> leave　arrive　call　go　visit　drink

1 What Susan really likes is ＿＿cycling[to cycle]＿＿ .
Susan이 정말로 좋아하는 것은 자전거 타기이다.

2 I finished ＿＿＿＿＿＿＿＿ the dishes.
나는 설거지를 끝냈다.

3 He can keep ＿＿＿＿＿＿＿＿ here.
그는 여기서 계속 일할 수 있다.

4 He stopped ＿＿＿＿＿＿＿＿ and fell asleep.
그는 글쓰기를 멈추고 잠이 들었다.

5 He avoids ＿＿＿＿＿＿＿＿ about Linda.
그는 Linda에 대해 말하기를 꺼린다.

6 Katie chose ＿＿＿＿＿＿＿＿ by train.
Katie는 기차를 타고 가기로 정했다.

7 Would you mind ＿＿＿＿＿＿＿＿ that again?
그거 다시 한 번 설명해 주시겠어요?

8 I wish ＿＿＿＿＿＿＿＿ you again.
제가 다음에 당신을 또 방문할 수 있으면 좋겠습니다.

9 I hate ＿＿＿＿＿＿＿＿ home.
나는 집을 떠나기가 싫다.

10 I need ＿＿＿＿＿＿＿＿ some coffee.
나는 커피를 좀 마셔야겠다.

11 They hope ＿＿＿＿＿＿＿＿ around two o'clock.
그들은 2시경에 도착할 것으로 기대한다.

12 He promised ＿＿＿＿＿＿＿＿ me tonight.
그는 오늘밤에 내게 전화하기로 약속했다.

B 사진을 보고 주어진 단어를 빈칸에 알맞은 형태로 쓰세요. (한 단어로 쓰세요.)

1 ______Swimming______ is fun. (swim)
수영은 재미있다.

2 __________________ is exciting. (ski)
스키를 타는 것은 신난다.

3 Her hobby is __________________ movies. (watch)
그녀의 취미는 영화를 보는 것이다.

4 __________________ a sandwich is fun. (make)
샌드위치를 만드는 것은 재미있다.

5 I enjoy __________________ basketball. (play)
나는 농구하는 것을 즐긴다.

6 __________________ is good for your body. (walk)
걷기는 몸에 좋다.

A 우리말과 같은 뜻이 되도록 주어진 말을 바르게 배열하세요.

1 비행기 여행은 신난다. (by / airplane / traveling)

→ _______Traveling by airplane_______ is exciting.

2 그는 스포츠를 즐겨본다. (watching / enjoys / sports)

→ He _______________________.

3 가장 좋은 취미 중 하나는 음악을 듣는 것이다. (music / to / listening)

→ One of the best hobbies is _______________________.

4 수영은 건강에 좋다. (good / swimming / is / for)

→ _______________________ your health.

5 그는 실수하는 것을 싫어한다. (making / hates / mistakes)

→ He _______________________.

6 아이들과 일하는 게 즐거우세요? (working / enjoy / with)

→ Do you _______________________ children?

7 영어로 쓰는 것은 쉽지 않다. (English / in / writing)

→ _______________________ is not easy.

8 그녀는 공부하는 것을 좋아하지 않는다. (like / doesn't / studying)

→ She _______________________.

9 Tom은 축구 하는 것을 정말 좋아한다. (playing / loves / soccer)

→ Tom really _______________________.

10 그녀는 2년 전에 가르치는 것을 그만두었다. (gave / teaching / up)

→ She _______________________ two years ago.

ⓑ 밑줄 친 부분을 바르게 고쳐 문장을 다시 쓰세요.

1 Do you mind to turn down the music?   음악 소리 좀 낮춰 줄래요?

→ _Do you mind turning down the music?_

2 She needs feel loved.   그녀는 사랑받는다고 느끼는 것이 필요하다.

→ ____

3 I enjoy to visiting new places.   나는 새로운 곳을 방문하는 것을 즐긴다.

→ ____

4 He keeps try to talk to me.   그는 계속 내게 말을 걸려고 한다.

→ ____

5 Did you finish to read this book?   너는 이 책을 다 읽었니?

→ ____

6 Stop to talking and listen!   이야기 그만하고 잘 들어라!

→ ____

7 What do you want doing tomorrow?   너는 내일 무엇을 하고 싶니?

→ ____

8 I'm planning staying here.   나는 여기에 머무를 계획이다.

→ ____

9 He needs to losing a pound or two.   그는 몸무게를 1~2 파운드 줄일 필요가 있다.

→ ____

10 I was hoping leave work early today.   나는 오늘 일찍 퇴근하길 바라고 있었다.

→ ____

A 우리말과 같은 뜻이 되도록 주어진 말을 이용하여 문장을 완성하세요.

1 그의 취미는 농구를 하는 것이다. (hobby, playing, is, basketball)

→ His hobby is playing basketball.

2 그녀는 매일 걷는 것을 즐긴다. (walking, daily, enjoys)

→ ____

3 나는 일주일에 한 번 수영하러 간다. (go, swimming, once, a week)

→ ____

4 나는 내 숙제를 하는 게 싫다. (doing, hate, homework)

→ ____

5 문을 열어도 될까요? (would, mind, the door, opening)

→ ____

6 그들은 달리기 시작했다. (started, to run)

→ ____

7 나는 기차를 기다리는 게 싫다. (hate, to wait, for, the train)

→ ____

8 내 방을 청소하는 것은 지루하다. (cleaning, room, boring)

→ ____

9 나는 설거지를 끝냈다. (doing, finished, the dishes)

→ ____

10 그는 등산을 좋아한다. (like, mountains, climbing)

→ ____

B 어법상 **틀린** 부분을 찾아 문장을 다시 쓰세요.

1 I keep to make the same mistake. 나는 같은 실수를 계속한다.

→ I keep making the same mistake.

2 Would you mind to exchange seats? 자리를 바꿀 수 있을까요?

→ _______________________________

3 I want being alone. 나는 혼자 있고 싶다.

→ _______________________________

4 They hope succeeding. 그들은 성공하기를 기대한다.

→ _______________________________

5 Mr. Jones wishes seeing you. Jones씨가 당신을 보기를 원한다.

→ _______________________________

6 I plan to going fishing. 나는 낚시하러 갈 계획이다.

→ _______________________________

7 We chose to going by bus. 우리는 버스로 가기로 정했다.

→ _______________________________

8 She decided growing her hair. 그녀는 머리를 기르기로 결정했다.

→ _______________________________

9 He promised coming back. 그는 돌아오겠다고 약속했다.

→ _______________________________

10 I like to climbing mountains. 나는 등산을 좋아한다.

→ _______________________________

LEVEL UP

 A 우리말과 같은 뜻이 되도록 빈칸에 알맞은 말을 쓰세요.

1 _____Riding_____ _____a_____ _____bike_____ is exciting.
자전거 타기는 신난다.

2 _______________ _______________ _______________ is difficult.
영어로 쓰는 것은 어렵다.

3 Do you _______________ _______________ in the forest?
너는 숲속에서 걷는 걸 즐기니?

4 Did you _______________ _______________ that magazine?
너는 저 잡지를 다 읽었니?

5 He can _______________ _______________ for an hour.
그는 한 시간 동안 달리기를 계속할 수 있다.

6 I _______________ washing _______________ _______________.
나는 설거지 하는 것을 싫어한다.

B 우리말과 같은 뜻이 되도록 빈칸에 알맞은 말을 쓰세요.

1 All my family ___________ enjoy ___________ ___________ skiing ___________.
우리 가족은 모두 스키 타기를 즐긴다.

2 ___________________ _________________ with your food!
음식 가지고 장난 그만해라!

3 For him, __________________ ________________ is a simple thing to do.
그에게는 친구를 사귀는 일이 하기 쉬운 것이다.

4 ________________ is the best form of ________________.
가르치는 일은 배움의 가장 좋은 형태이다.

5 I ________________ ________________ twice a week.
나는 일주일에 두 번 수영하러 간다.

6 I try to ____________ ____________ ____________ on Saturdays.
나는 토요일에 쇼핑하러 가는 것을 피하려고 한다.

7 He ______________ ____________ ____________ some weight.
그는 몸무게를 좀 줄일 필요가 있다.

8 I'm not _______ ________ _________ here for long.
나는 여기에 오래 머무를 계획이 없다.

9 He keeps ____________ ____________ ____________ games.
그는 게임을 이기려고 계속 노력한다.

10 I ____________ ____________ ____________.
나는 사람들을 만나는 것을 즐긴다.

11 Most people ____________ ____________ ____________ loved.
대부분의 사람들은 사랑받는다고 느끼는 것이 필요하다.

12 Do you ____________ ____________ ____________ the volume a little?
볼륨을 약간 줄여도 괜찮을까요?

[1~3] (   ) 안에서 알맞은 것을 고르세요.

1 His hobby is (① to watching / ② watching) movies.

2 (① Make / ② Making) a sandwich is fun.

3 They can keep (① to work / ② working) here.

4 어법상 올바른 문장을 고르세요.

① He finished to wash the dishes.

② He avoided to talk about Susan.

③ He hates leaving home.

④ He chose to going by train.

5 밑줄 친 부분을 바르게 고친 것을 고르세요.

He stopped <u>to writing</u> and fell asleep.

① writing   ② written   ③ write   ④ wrote

6 밑줄 친 부분이 <u>어색한</u> 것을 고르세요.

① Would you mind <u>explaining</u> that again?

② They hope <u>arriving</u> around three o'clock.

③ I wish <u>to visit</u> you again.

④ I need <u>to talk</u> to someone.

7 밑줄 친 부분의 쓰임이 나머지와 <u>다른</u> 것을 고르세요.

① I enjoy <u>travelling</u>.

② He is <u>playing</u> tennis right now.

③ Dad gave up <u>smoking</u>.

④ She avoids <u>making</u> a decision.

[8~9] 빈칸에 들어갈 수 <u>없는</u> 말을 고르세요.

8   He didn't ______________ to go there.

① want   ② plan   ③ promise   ④ mind

9   Making friends ______________.

① isn't difficult   ② is interesting

③ is exciting   ④ aren't easy

10 빈칸에 공통으로 알맞은 말을 고르세요.

· She _____________ playing the piano.
· The girl _____________ to cry.

① began   ② avoided   ③ gave up   ④ finished

11 빈칸에 들어갈 말이 바르게 짝지어진 것을 고르세요.

· The boy kept _____________. (cry)
· Mom promised _____________ shopping with me. (go)

① crying – going   ② to cry – going

③ crying – to go   ④ to cry – to go

12 밑줄 친 부분이 올바른 것을 고르세요.

① She doesn't like to studying.

② He quit to work here.

③ He gave up to teach two years ago.

④ He promised to call me tonight.

13 우리말을 영어로 바르게 옮긴 것을 고르세요.

이야기 그만하고 잘 들어봐!

① Stop to talk and listen!

② Stop talking and listen!

③ Stop to talk and listening!

④ Stop talking and listening!

14 어법상 <u>틀린</u> 부분을 찾아 바르게 고쳐 쓰세요.

> He gave up to smoke two years ago.

_______________________ ➡ _______________________

15 두 문장이 같은 의미가 되도록 주어진 단어를 빈칸에 알맞은 형태로 쓰세요.

> Do you mind (1) _____________ on the light? (turn)
> I want (2) _____________ on the light. (turn)

(1) _____________________   (2) _____________________

16 이메일을 보고 주어진 단어를 이용하여 빈칸에 알맞은 말을 쓰세요.

New message   _ ⌐ ×

To
Subject

Hi Susan,

Do you like _____________ _____________ movies? (watch)
I enjoy _____________ to the movies. (go)
I want _____________ _____________ a movie this afternoon. (see)
But I hate _____________ there alone. (go)
Do you have time?

David

Send

실전 Test 01회

[1~2] 밑줄 친 부분의 쓰임이 나머지와 다른 것을 고르세요.

1
① He likes to play basketball.

② I want to go to the soccer field.

③ She learned to ride a bike.

④ It's time to go home.

2
① His hobby is swimming.

② She is swimming right now.

③ Swimming in the river is fun.

④ Every student likes swimming.

3 밑줄 친 부분의 쓰임이 보기 와 같은 것을 고르세요.

> 보기 She saved money to buy a bike.

① It is wrong to tell a lie.

② I went there to see Peter.

③ It is time to go to school.

④ He doesn't have anything to wear.

[4~5] 빈칸에 들어갈 수 없는 말을 고르세요.

4
    _______ is fun.

① Sing
② Singing

③ Dancing
④ To dance

5
    She ______ to play the violin.

① began
② liked

③ finished
④ wanted

6 우리말을 영어로 바르게 옮긴 것을 고르세요.

> 그는 자기 방 청소하는 것을 싫어한다.

① He hates cleaning his room.

② He hates to cleaning his room.

③ He doesn't like clean his room.

④ He doesn't like to cleaning his room.

7 두 문장이 같은 의미가 되도록 빈칸에 알맞은 말을 고르세요.

> She likes climbing mountains.
> → She likes ______ mountains.

① climb ② to climb

③ to climbing ④ for climbing

[8~9] 빈칸에 알맞은 말을 고르세요.

8 She ______ going shopping.

① wants ② hopes

③ enjoys ④ decides

9 They stopped ______.

① sing ② working

③ to singing ④ to working

10 어법상 올바른 문장을 고르세요.

① His goal is to being a pianist.

② He practices hard becoming a pianist.

③ She doesn't have the money buy the car.

④ My sister will go to Paris to study French.

[11~12] 어법상 <u>틀린</u> 문장을 고르세요.

11 ① I decided for buy it.

② His job is to build houses.

③ Her dream is to become a writer.

④ It's exciting to watch soccer games.

12 ① Cooking pasta is his job.

② Running fast is not easy.

③ Watering flowers are fun.

④ I really love skating.

13 밑줄 친 부분이 어색한 것을 고르세요.

① It's time to go to bed.

② I have some work to finish.

③ We bought some fruit to make a salad.

④ They will go to the park to playing soccer.

[14~15] 밑줄 친 부분을 바르게 고친 것을 고르세요.

14
> He needs buy an umbrella.

① to buy   ② to buying

③ bought   ④ for buy

15
> - She ran catch the last bus.
> - He wanted to avoid meet her.

① to catch — meeting

② to catch — to meet

③ catching — to meet

④ catching — meeting

[16~17] 빈칸에 들어갈 말이 바르게 짝지어진 것을 고르세요.

16
> - It is not easy ________ across the river.
> - I went to the river ________ the birds.

① swimming — seeing

② to swim — to see

③ swim — to see

④ to swim — see

17
> - The baby kept ________.
> - Dad promised ________ fishing with me.

① crying — going

② to cry — going

③ crying — to go

④ to cry — to go

18 빈칸에 공통으로 알맞은 말을 고르세요.

> They decided ________ a fire.
> He went to the city ________ money.

① make   ② to make

③ making   ④ to making

19 우리말과 같은 뜻이 되도록 주어진 말을 바르게 배열하세요.

> 강에서 수영하는 것은 위험하다.
> (it / dangerous / is / to / in the river / swim / .)

____

20 어법상 틀린 부분을 찾아 바르게 고쳐 쓰세요.

> I don't mind to wait for a few minutes.

________________ ➡ ________________

21 두 문장의 의미를 to부정사를 이용하여 한 문장으로 나타내세요.

> Jenny practices playing piano.
> +
> She will become a great pianist.

➡ Jenny practices playing piano

______________________________________ .

22 그림을 보고 주어진 단어를 이용하여 빈칸에 알맞은 말을 쓰세요.

> My brother and I are too different.
> I enjoy __________ a bike. (ride)
> It is fun __________ __________ a bike. (ride)
> My brother likes __________ __________ a book. (read)
> His dream is __________ __________ a writer. (become)
> Today I woke up early __________ __________ to the soccer field. (go)
> But my brother hates __________ __________ early. (get up)
> He just wants something __________ __________ . (read)

Chapter 03

전치사

학습목표

1 시간을 나타내는 전치사에 대해 알아보아요.
2 장소를 나타내는 전치사에 대해 알아보아요.
3 방향을 나타내는 전치사에 대해 알아보아요.
4 그 외의 다양한 의미로 쓰이는 전치사에 대해 알아보아요.

모르는 단어에 체크해 보세요.

church
교회

vacation
휴가

pyramid
피라미드

clap
박수를 치다

soldier
군인

wallet
지갑

pillow
베개

gym
체육관

potato
감자

hunter
사냥꾼

ladder
사다리

eagle
독수리

glasses
안경

balloon
풍선

bakery
제과점

desert
사막

pear
배

pumpkin
호박

mosquito
모기

butterfly
나비

시간의 전치사

- 명사나 대명사 앞에 놓여서 시간이나 장소, 방향 등을 나타내는 말을 전치사라고 해요.

전치사 + 명사(대명사)	**at** six 여섯 시에 (시간)　　　**in** the library 도서관에서 (장소) **across** the river 강을 건너서 (방향)

- 전치사 at, on, in은 명사나 대명사 앞에 놓여서 시간을 나타낼 때 쓰여요. 모두 '~에'라는 뜻이지만, 그 쓰임은 각각 달라요.

at + 시간/특정 시점	**on** + 날짜/요일/특정한 날	**in** + 오전[오후]/연도/월/계절
at 7 o'clock 7시 정각에 **at** 10:30 10시 30분에 **at** night 밤에 **at** breakfast 아침 식사에	**on** October 7 10월 7일에 **on** Sunday 일요일에 **on** my birthday 내 생일에 **on** New Year's Day 설날에	**in** the morning 아침에 **in** 2021 2021년에 **in** August 8월에 **in** summer 여름에

I got up **at** 6 o'clock. 나는 6시에 일어났다.
They go to church **on** Sunday. 그들은 일요일에 교회에 간다.
My sister was born **in** 2015. 내 여동생은 2015년에 태어났다.

- during과 for는 둘 다 '~ 동안'을 뜻하지만, during은 '언제(when)' 그 일이 일어났는지를 말할 때 쓰이고, for는 '얼마 동안(how long)' 그 일이 계속되었는지를 말할 때 쓰여요.

during + 시기 (언제)	**for** + 기간 (얼마 동안)
during the vacation 방학 동안	**for** three months 3개월 동안

Don't talk **during** the exam. 시험 중에는 말을 하지 마라.
It rained **for** two hours. 두 시간 동안 비가 내렸다.

- until과 by는 둘 다 '~까지'를 의미하지만, until은 언제까지 '계속'되는 것을 말할 때 쓰이고, by는 '~보다 늦지 않게(no later than)'라는 뜻으로 말할 때 쓰여요.

A: Can I stay **until** the weekend? 내가 주말까지 머물러도 되니? (주말까지 계속)
B: Yes, but you have to leave **by** ten on Monday.
응, 하지만 월요일 10시까지는 떠나야 해. (늦어도 월요일 10시까지는)

CHECK UP

정답 및 해설 p.6

A 빈칸에 들어갈 말로 알맞은 것을 고르세요.

1 ___________ 9 p.m. 오후 9시에 　　ⓐ at　　ⓑ in

2 ___________ lunch 점심 때 　　ⓐ at　　ⓑ on

3 ___________ Wednesday 수요일에 　　ⓐ at　　ⓑ on

4 ___________ summer 여름에 　　ⓐ on　　ⓑ in

5 ___________ my birthday 내 생일에 　　ⓐ on　　ⓑ in

6 ___________ the morning 아침에 　　ⓐ on　　ⓑ in

B 사진을 보고 알맞은 말에 V 표시하세요.

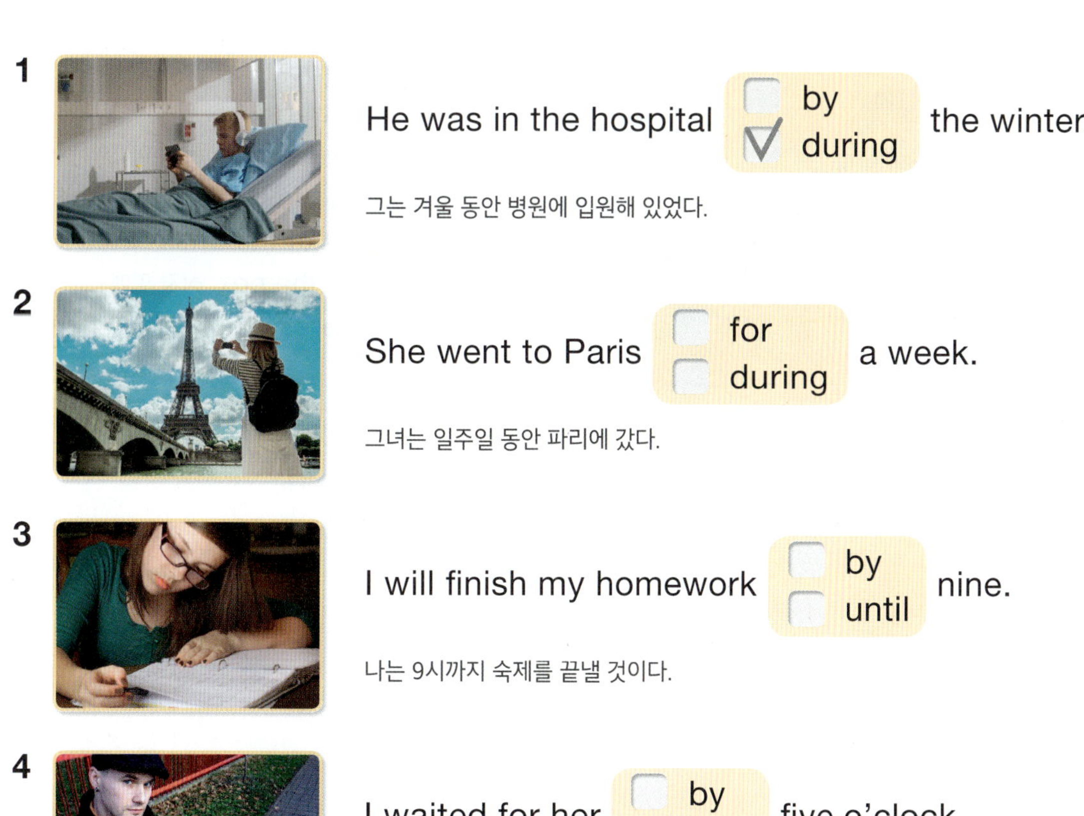

1 He was in the hospital ☐ by ☑ during the winter.

그는 겨울 동안 병원에 입원해 있었다.

2 She went to Paris ☐ for ☐ during a week.

그녀는 일주일 동안 파리에 갔다.

3 I will finish my homework ☐ by ☐ until nine.

나는 9시까지 숙제를 끝낼 것이다.

4 I waited for her ☐ by ☐ until five o'clock.

나는 그녀를 5시까지 기다렸다.

장소의 전치사

● 장소의 전치사 in은 도시, 국가와 같은 큰 장소를 나타내는 말 앞에 쓰이고, at은 비교적 좁은 장소 앞에 쓰여요.

in + 장소, 공간 (~에, ~에서)	at + 한 지점 (~에, ~에서)
in New York 뉴욕에서 **in** Italy 이탈리아에서	**at** a bus stop 버스 정류장에서 **at** the hotel 호텔에서

My uncle lives **in** Paris. 내 삼촌은 파리에 사신다.

We bought tickets **at** the station. 우리는 역에서 표를 샀다.

● 위치를 나타내는 전치사에는 in, on, behind, in front of, under, next, between 등이 있어요.

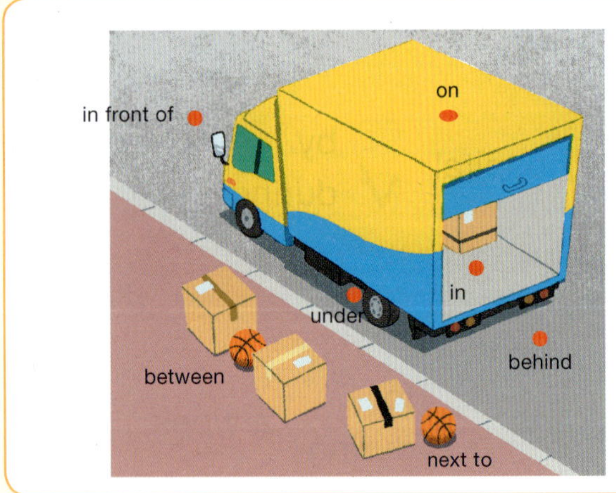

in the truck 트럭 안에
on the truck 트럭 위에
under the truck 트럭 아래에
behind the truck 트럭 뒤에
in front of the truck 트럭 앞에
next to the box 상자 옆에
between the boxes 상자들 사이에

A doll is **in** the box. 인형이 상자 안에 있다.

A vase is **on** the table. 꽃병이 탁자 위에 있다.

There is a dog **under** the table. 그 탁자 아래에 개 한 마리가 있다.

A boy is **behind** the tree. 나무 뒤에 한 남자아이가 있다.

A duck is **between** the trees. 그 나무들 사이에 오리 한 마리가 있다.

Tip ・ 전치사 뒤에 대명사가 올 때는 반드시 목적격을 써요.

between they (X) ➞ between **them** (O)   next to she (X) ➞ next to **her** (O)

CHECK UP

A 우리말과 같은 뜻이 되도록 (　) 안에서 알맞은 것을 고르세요.

1 There are many pyramids (at / (in)) Egypt.　이집트에는 많은 피라미드들이 있다.

2 Let's meet (at / in) the bus stop.　버스 정류장에서 만나자.

3 What did you do (at / in) school today?　너는 오늘 학교에서 무엇을 했니?

4 I bought two books (at / on) the bookstore.　나는 서점에서 책을 두 권 샀다.

5 Jenny and Fred live (at / in) Seoul.　Jenny와 Fred는 서울에 산다.

6 Which is the largest city (at / in) the world?　세계에서 가장 큰 도시는 어느 것이니?

B 사진을 보고 (　) 안에서 알맞은 것을 고르세요.

1 

He is (under / (behind)) his daughter.

2 

Some apples are (in / over) the basket.

3 

The child is (between / behind) her parents.

4 

He is (in / in front of) the fire.

5 

A dog is sleeping (under / in) the bed.

6 

They are (next to / between) the tree.

A 빈칸에 in, at, on 중 알맞은 전치사를 쓰세요.

1 Picasso was born ______in______ 1881. 피카소는 1881년에 태어났다.

2 She has an English class __________ Thursday. 그녀는 목요일에 영어 수업이 있다.

3 They will go shopping __________ the weekend. 그들은 주말에 쇼핑을 갈 것이다.

4 I don't eat snacks __________ night. 나는 밤에 간식을 먹지 않는다.

5 Tom gets up early __________ the morning. Tom은 아침에 일찍 일어난다.

6 She usually goes to bed __________ 10. 그녀는 보통 10시에 잔다.

B 우리말과 같은 뜻이 되도록 보기 에서 알맞은 전치사를 골라 쓰세요.

보기	on	in	during	for	by	until

1 I don't watch TV ________in________ the evening.
나는 저녁에 TV를 보지 않는다.

2 The barber slept ________________ lunchtime.
그 이발사는 점심시간 동안 잠을 잤다.

3 You should finish your homework ________________ Wednesday.
너는 수요일까지 숙제를 끝내야 한다.

4 They were clapping ________________ 10 minutes.
그들은 10분 동안 박수를 치고 있었다.

5 I clean my bedroom ________________ Saturday.
나는 토요일에 내 침실을 청소한다.

6 Let's wait ________________ next week.
다음 주까지 기다리자.

정답 및 해설 p.6

A 우리말과 같은 뜻이 되도록 알맞은 것을 고르세요.

1 런던에	(in) / on	London
2 나무 아래에	on / under	the tree
3 TV 앞에	behind / in front of	the TV
4 식당에서	at / on	the restaurant
5 침대 위에	on / over	the bed

B 사진을 보고 보기 에서 알맞은 말을 골라 쓰세요.

보기	behind	between	next to	under

1 

A baby is sleeping ______between______ the parents.

아기가 부모 사이에서 자고 있다.

2 

A cat is ________________ the table.

고양이가 탁자 밑에 있다.

3 

A boy is hiding ________________ the tree.

한 소년이 나무 뒤에 숨어 있다.

4 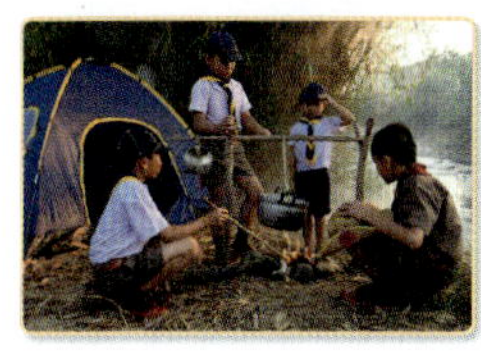

There are children ________________ the tent.

텐트 옆에 아이들이 있다.

A 우리말과 같은 뜻이 되도록 보기 에서 알맞은 전치사를 골라 쓰세요. (중복 사용 가능)

> 보기   at   on   in   for   by   until

1 My sister was born _____in_____ 2012.
내 여동생은 2012년에 태어났다.

2 Please wait for me here _____________ 7 o'clock.
7시까지 여기서 저를 기다려 주세요.

3 Summer vacation starts _____________ July 15.
여름방학은 7월 15일에 시작한다.

4 There are many flowers here _____________ the spring.
여기는 봄에 많은 꽃들이 있다.

5 _____________ night, you can see the stars.
밤에는 별을 볼 수 있다.

6 I have to finish the work _____________ Friday.
나는 금요일까지 그 일을 끝내야 한다.

7 Let's wait _____________ the morning.
아침까지 기다리자.

8 I visited my grandmother _____________ New Year's Day.
나는 설날에 할머니를 찾아뵈었다.

9 We cleaned the garden _____________ two hours.
우리는 두 시간 동안 정원을 청소했다.

10 We had snow _____________ November last year.
작년에는 11월에 눈이 왔다.

11 I have a history class _____________ 9 o'clock.
나는 9시에 역사 수업이 있다.

12 Bake the cake _____________ 40 minutes.
케이크를 40분간 구우세요.

B 우리말과 같은 뜻이 되도록 (   ) 안에서 알맞은 것을 고르세요.

1 There is an umbrella (in / at) the box.
상자 속에 우산이 있다.

2 The soldier sat (under / on) the bench.
그 군인은 벤치 위에 앉았다.

3 A lion is sitting (behind / next to) a rock.
사자가 바위 옆에 앉아 있다.

4 A fly is sitting (on / at) the wall.
벽 위에 파리가 한 마리 앉아 있다.

5 A ship passes (behind / between) the two islands.
두 섬 사이로 배 한 척이 지나간다.

6 She left her umbrella (at / in) home.
그녀는 집에 우산을 두고 왔다.

7 A dog is lying (under / next to) the table.
개 한 마리가 탁자 아래 누워 있다.

8 There is a small hill (on / behind) the house.
그 집 뒤에 작은 언덕이 있다.

9 The bus stops (in front of / between) the market.
그 버스는 시장 앞에 선다.

10 She doesn't have any money (in / at) her wallet.
그녀의 지갑 안에는 돈이 하나도 없다.

11 The children are swimming (over / under) the bridge.
아이들이 다리 아래서 수영을 하고 있다.

12 A cat is lying (behind / next to) the pillow.
고양이 한 마리가 베개 옆에 누워 있다.

STEP UP 2

A 우리말과 같은 뜻이 되도록 빈칸에 알맞은 전치사를 쓰세요.

1 사흘 동안 비가 내렸다.

→ It rained _____for_____ three days.

2 나는 이 과학 숙제를 내일까지 끝내야 해.

→ I must finish this science homework _____________ tomorrow.

3 나는 오후에 슈퍼마켓에 갔다.

→ I went to the supermarket _____________ the afternoon.

4 그녀는 일요일에 많은 선물을 받았다.

→ She got a lot of gifts _____________ Sunday.

5 나는 오후 5시까지 수학을 공부할 거야.

→ I'm going to study math _____________ 5 p.m.

6 나는 영화를 보는 중에 전화를 받았다.

→ I received a phone call _____________ the movie.

7 자동차 앞에 고양이 한 마리가 있다.

→ There is a cat _____________ the car.

8 농부가 나무들 사이에 앉아 있다.

→ A farmer is sitting _____________ the trees.

9 은행 옆에 체육관이 있다.

→ There is a gym _____________ the bank.

10 집 뒤에 작은 정원이 있다.

→ There is a small garden _____________ the house.

B 사진을 보고 at, on, in 중 알맞은 전치사를 골라 쓰세요.

1
We have lunch _______at_______ 12:30.
우리는 12시 30분에 점심을 먹는다.

2
They go to the sea _______________ the summer.
그들은 여름에 바다에 간다.

3
They drink tea _______________ breakfast.
그들은 아침 식사 때 차를 마신다.

4
We go to school _______________ weekdays.
우리는 평일에 학교에 간다.

5
Children wait for the school bus _______________ the bus stop.
아이들이 버스 정류장에서 스쿨버스를 기다린다.

6
There are a lot of ants _______________ the ground.
땅 위에 많은 개미들이 있다.

A 우리말과 같은 뜻이 되도록 주어진 말을 바르게 배열하세요.

1 나는 Fred를 오후 7시에 만났다. (Fred / met / seven / at)

→ I _______ met Fred at seven _______ p.m.

2 두 산 사이로 강이 흐른다. (the two / between / mountains)

→ A river flows _______________________________.

3 나는 토요일에 거실을 청소한다. (on / the living room / Saturday)

→ I clean _______________________________.

4 고래가 바다에서 헤엄치고 있다. (the / sea / in)

→ A whale is swimming _______________________________.

5 이 섬은 여름 동안 비가 많이 내린다. (during / summer / the)

→ It rains a lot on this island _______________________________.

6 벽에 그림이 있다. (the / on / wall)

→ There is a picture _______________________________.

7 밤에는 많은 별을 볼 수 있다. (at / many / night / stars)

→ You can see _______________________________.

8 내 고양이가 소파 뒤에 앉아 있다. (the / sofa / behind)

→ My cat is sitting _______________________________.

9 주말까지 머물러 있어도 되나요? (weekend / the / until)

→ Can I stay _______________________________?

10 그 버스는 병원 앞에 선다. (in / of / front / the hospital)

→ The bus stops _______________________________.

B 우리말과 같은 뜻이 되도록 주어진 말을 이용하여 문장을 완성하세요.

1 탁자 위에 많은 음식들이 있다. (the table)

→ There are many foods ______on the table______.

2 그 아기는 낮 동안에 잠을 많이 잔다. (the day)

→ The baby sleeps a lot ______________.

3 상자 뒤에 토끼 한 마리가 있다. (the box)

→ There is a rabbit ______________.

4 나는 10시에 수학 수업이 있다. (10 o'clock)

→ I have a math class ______________.

5 그 소녀는 나무 아래에서 기타를 연주하고 있다. (the tree)

→ The girl is playing the guitar ______________.

6 그녀는 프랑스에서 3년간 살았다. (three years)

→ She lived in France ______________.

7 내 자전거는 서점 앞에 있다. (the bookstore)

→ My bike is ______________.

8 그는 휴식하는 동안 만화책을 읽었다. (the break)

→ He read comic books ______________.

9 컴퓨터 옆에 프린터가 있다. (the computer)

→ There is a printer ______________.

10 두 건물 사이에 공원이 있다. (the two buildings)

→ There is a park ______________.

STEP UP 4

A 우리말과 같은 뜻이 되도록 주어진 말을 바르게 배열하세요.

1 그 박물관은 오후 5시에 문을 닫는다. (closes / at / the museum / 5 p.m.)

➡ The museum closes at 5 p.m.

2 네 모자 위에 새가 앉아 있어. (a bird / your hat / sitting / is / on / .)

➡ ______________________________________

3 아침 동안 비가 많이 내렸다. (during / it / a lot / the morning / rained / .)

➡ ______________________________________

4 다리 아래로 강물이 흐른다. (the river / the bridge / under / flows / .)

➡ ______________________________________

5 나는 토요일에 캠핑을 갈 것이다. (will / on / I / Saturday / go camping / .)

➡ ______________________________________

6 그 절 앞에 탑이 있다. (a tower / the temple / in front of / there is / .)

➡ ______________________________________

7 오후 3시까지 공부를 계속 해라. (until / keep studying / 3 p.m.)

➡ ______________________________________

8 두 도시 사이에 호수가 하나 있다. (the two cities / a lake / there is / between / .)

➡ ______________________________________

9 내 남동생은 2017년에 태어났다. (in 2017 / my younger brother / was born / .)

➡ ______________________________________

10 체육관 옆에 시장이 있다. (next to / a market / the gym / there is / .)

➡ ______________________________________

B 우리말과 같은 뜻이 되도록 밑줄 친 부분을 바르게 고쳐 문장을 다시 쓰세요.

1 There is a black cat <u>under</u> the roof. 지붕 위에 검은 고양이가 있다.

→ There is a black cat on the roof.

2 I get up <u>in</u> 7 every morning. 나는 매일 아침 7시에 일어난다.

→ ______________________________

3 There are some potatoes <u>on</u> the box. 상자 속에 감자가 몇 개 있다.

→ ______________________________

4 You can stay here <u>by</u> the weekend. 너는 주말까지 여기에 머물러도 돼.

→ ______________________________

5 There is a parking lot <u>in front of</u> the building. 그 건물 뒤에 주차장이 있다.

→ ______________________________

6 My father worked in Busan <u>during</u> a year. 내 아빠는 일 년 동안 부산에서 근무했다.

→ ______________________________

7 I want to get many gifts <u>in</u> Christmas. 나는 크리스마스에 많은 선물을 받고 싶어.

→ ______________________________

8 She is smiling <u>next to</u> her parents. 그녀는 부모님 사이에서 웃고 있다.

→ ______________________________

9 The hunter lived <u>on</u> the forest. 그 사냥꾼은 숲속에서 살았다.

→ ______________________________

10 He was born <u>at</u> August. 그는 8월에 태어났다.

→ ______________________________

LEVEL UP

A 우리말과 같은 뜻이 되도록 빈칸에 알맞은 말을 쓰세요.

1 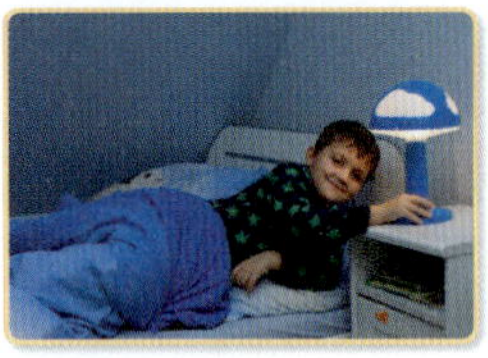

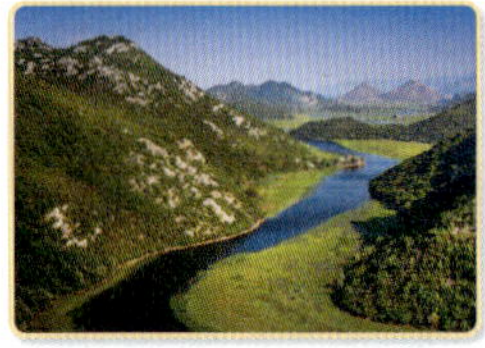

He goes to bed ____at____ 10.
그는 10시에 잠을 잔다.

2 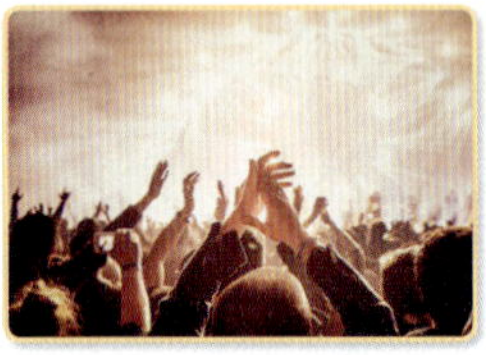

They were clapping ________ 3 minutes.
그들은 3분 동안 계속 박수를 쳤다.

3 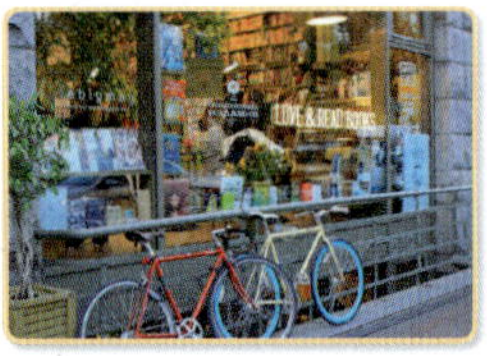

My bike is ________ the bookstore.
내 자전거는 서점 앞에 있다.

4 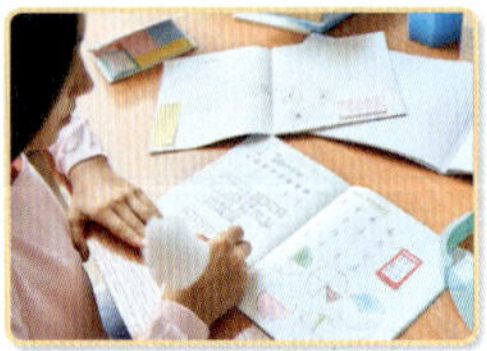

I'm going to study math ________ 5 p.m.
나는 오후 5시까지 수학을 공부할 거야.

5 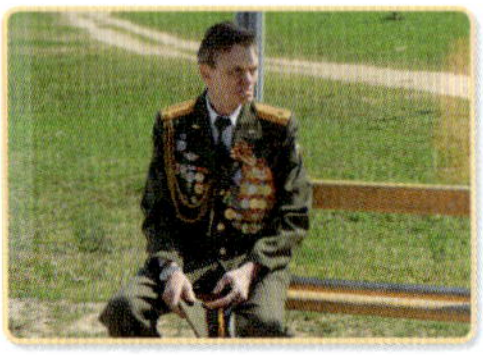

The soldier sat ________ the bench.
그 군인은 벤치 위에 앉았다.

6

A river flows ________ the two mountains.
두 산 사이로 강이 흐른다.

B 우리말과 같은 뜻이 되도록 빈칸에 알맞은 말을 쓰세요.

1 The post office is ___next___ ___to___ ___the___ ___library___.
우체국은 도서관 옆에 있다.

2 I will finish the homework ________________ ________________.
그 숙제를 목요일까지 마칠게요.

3 I don't watch TV ____________ ____________ ____________.
나는 저녁에 TV를 보지 않는다.

4 There is a small hill ____________ ____________ ____________.
그 집 뒤에 작은 언덕이 있다.

5 There are ____________ ____________ ____________ Egypt.
이집트에는 많은 피라미드가 있다.

6 We go to the sea ____________ ____________ ____________.
우리는 여름에 바다에 간다.

7 A dog is sleeping ____________ ____________ ____________.
개 한 마리가 침대 아래에서 자고 있다.

8 There are many flowers here ____________ ____________ ____________.
여기는 봄에 많은 꽃들이 있다.

9 There are a lot of ants ____________ ____________ ____________.
땅 위에 많은 개미들이 있다.

10 They arrived late ____________ ____________ ____________.
그들은 공항에 늦게 도착했다.

Unit 03

방향의 전치사

- '위로', '아래로' 등의 방향을 나타내는 말을 방향의 전치사라고 해요.

방향 전치사	의미	쓰임
up	~ 위로	**up** the ladder 사다리 위로
down	~ 아래로	**down** the stairs 계단 아래로
from (+ 출발지)	~에서, ~으로부터	**from** home 집에서
to (+ 도착지)	~로, ~에	**to** the park 공원으로
across	~을 가로질러	**across** the road 도로를 가로질러
through	~을 통과해서	**through** the village 마을을 통과해서

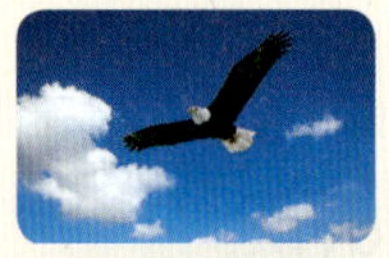

An eagle is flying high **up** in the sky. 독수리가 하늘 위로 높이 날고 있다.

He is climbing **up** the ladder. 그가 사다리 위로 오르고 있다.

A shooting star is falling **down**. 별똥별이 아래로 떨어지고 있다.

She is coming **down** the stairs. 그녀가 계단 아래로 내려오고 있다.

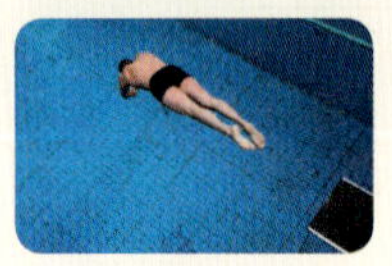

He jumped down **from** the diving board. 그는 다이빙대에서 뛰어내렸다.

I walked here **from** home. 나는 집에서 여기로 걸어왔다.

I usually walk **to** school.   나는 보통 걸어서 학교에 간다.

An apple fell **to** the ground. 사과 한 개가 땅으로 떨어졌다.

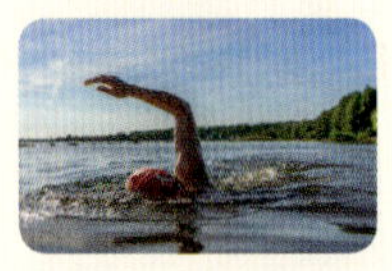

He is swimming **across** the river. 그는 강을 가로질러 헤엄치고 있다.

He ran **across** the road. 그는 도로를 가로질러 뛰었다.

The train is going **through** the tunnel. 기차가 터널을 통과하고 있다.

She drove **through** the village. 그녀는 마을을 통과해서 차를 몰았다.

Tip from과 to는 종종 결합해서 from A to B의 형태로 쓰여, 'A에서 B로', 'A부터 B까지'의 의미를 나타내요.
I went **from** Seoul **to** Rome by plane.   나는 비행기로 서울에서 로마로 갔다.
The store is open **from** 11 a.m. **to** 9 p.m. 그 상점은 오전 11시부터 오후 9시까지 문을 연다.

정답 및 해설 p.7

A 우리말과 같은 뜻이 되도록 (   ) 안에서 알맞은 것을 고르세요.

1 An iguana is climbing (on / up) the wall.   이구아나가 벽을 올라가고 있다.

2 He ran (over / across) the square.   그는 광장을 가로질러 달렸다.

3 They are coming (down / to) the hill.   그들은 언덕을 내려오고 있다.

4 My family will go (to / at) the zoo.   우리 가족은 동물원에 갈 것이다.

5 A fly came in (from / through) the hole.   파리가 구멍을 통해 들어왔다.

6 An orange fell (to / from) the tree.   오렌지가 나무에서 떨어졌다.

B 사진에 알맞은 말을 연결하세요.

1 

2 

3 

4 

ⓐ high up in the sky
하늘 높이

ⓑ across the street
도로를 건너서

ⓒ through the glasses
안경을 통해서

ⓓ to the island
섬으로

04

기타 전치사

● 전치사는 문장에 따라 다양한 의미로 쓰일 수 있어요.

방향 전치사	의미	쓰임
with	~와 함께, ~를 가진	**with** you 너와 함께
without	~ 없이	**without** her help 그녀의 도움 없이
like	~같이, ~처럼	**like** a star 별처럼
about	~에 관해, 대략	**about** your dream 너의 꿈에 대해
by (+ 교통수단)	~를 타고	**by** train 기차를 타고

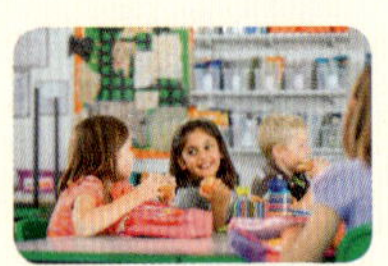

She had lunch **with** her friends. 그녀는 친구들과 함께 점심을 먹었다.

Look at the girl **with** blond hair. 금발머리를 가진 소녀를 보세요.

He went out **without** an umbrella. 그는 우산 없이 외출했다.

He did it **without** her help. 그는 그녀의 도움 없이 그 일을 했다.

The baby smiles **like** an angel. 그 아기는 천사처럼 웃는다.

A starfish looks **like** a star. 불가사리는 별처럼 생겼다.

She is reading a book **about** animals. 그녀는 동물들에 관한 책을 읽고 있다.

He slept for **about** two hours. 그는 대략 두 시간 동안 잤다.

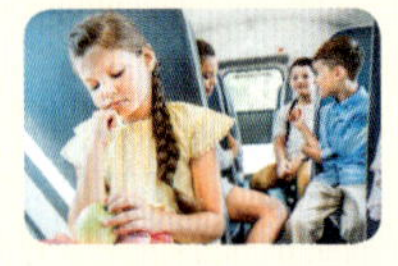

She goes to school **by** bus. 그녀는 버스를 타고 학교에 다닌다.

My uncle went to Paris **by** airplane. 나의 삼촌은 비행기로 파리에 갔다.

Tip on foot은 '걸어서, 도보로'라는 뜻이에요.

Many students go to school **on foot**. 많은 학생들이 걸어서 학교에 간다.

A 전치사와 우리말 뜻을 연결하세요.

1	by
2	like
3	with
4	without
5	about

ⓐ ~ 없이
ⓑ ~에 관해
ⓒ ~를 타고
ⓓ ~처럼
ⓔ ~를 가진

B 사진을 보고 알맞은 전치사에 V 표시하세요.

1 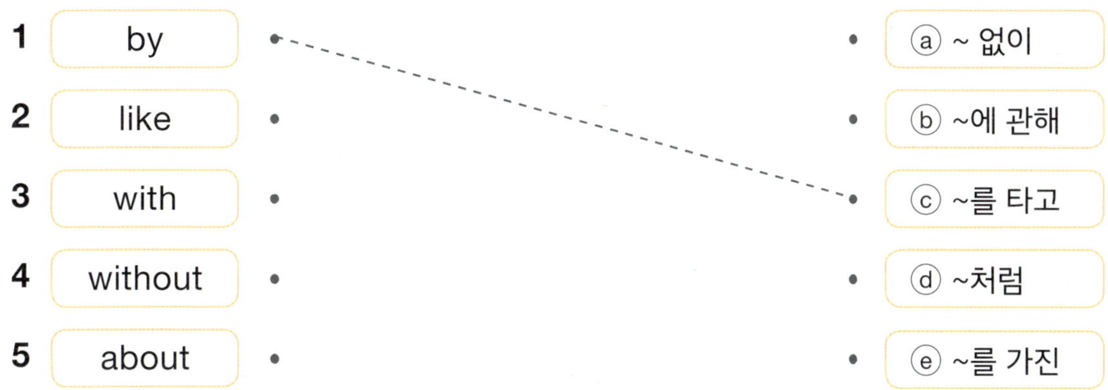

We can't live ☐ by / ☑ without love.

우리는 사랑 없이는 살 수 없다.

2 

It takes 10 hours ☐ with / ☐ by airplane.

비행기로 10시간이 걸린다.

3

He looks ☐ about / ☐ like a bear.

그는 곰처럼 생겼다.

4

She wrote an essay ☐ about / ☐ without a cat.

그녀는 고양이에 관한 수필을 썼다.

A 우리말과 일치하는 문장을 고르세요.

1 우리는 우체국에 가는 중이다.
- ⓐ We are going to the post office.
- ⓑ We are going from the post office.

2 풍선이 땅으로 내려오고 있다.
- ⓐ A balloon is coming across to the ground.
- ⓑ A balloon is coming down to the ground.

3 개구리가 개울을 가로질러 헤엄친다.
- ⓐ A frog swims through the stream.
- ⓑ A frog swims across the stream.

4 꿀벌이 꽃에서 꽃으로 날아다닌다.
- ⓐ Bees fly from flower to flower.
- ⓑ Bees fly from flower and flower.

5 불빛이 창문을 통해 들어왔다.
- ⓐ The light came down the window.
- ⓑ The light came through the window.

B 우리말과 같은 뜻이 되도록 알맞은 전치사를 보기 에서 골라 쓰세요.

> 보기   up   down   from   to   across   through

1 The bakery is ______across______ the street.
제과점은 길 건너편에 있다.

2 The truck is going ______________ the hill.
트럭이 언덕을 올라가고 있다.

3 Sunlight comes in ______________ the hole.
구멍을 통해 햇빛이 들어온다.

4 The train runs ______________ Seoul ______________ Busan.
그 기차는 서울에서 부산까지 운행한다.

5 The children went ______________ to the first floor.
아이들은 1층으로 내려갔다.

정답 및 해설 p.7

A 우리말과 같은 뜻이 되도록 알맞은 것을 고르세요.

1	물 없이	with / (without)	water
2	강아지처럼	like / about	the puppy
3	배를 타고	by / with	ship
4	걸어서	across / on	foot
5	푸른 눈을 가진	about / with	blue eyes

B 사진을 보고 보기 에서 알맞은 전치사를 골라 쓰세요.

보기	about	like	by	without

1 

She studied ______about______ monkeys.

그녀는 원숭이에 관해 연구했다.

2 

He is walking in the desert ______________ a hat.

그는 모자 없이 사막을 걷고 있다.

3 

She went to London ______________ airplane.

그녀는 비행기를 타고 런던에 갔다.

4 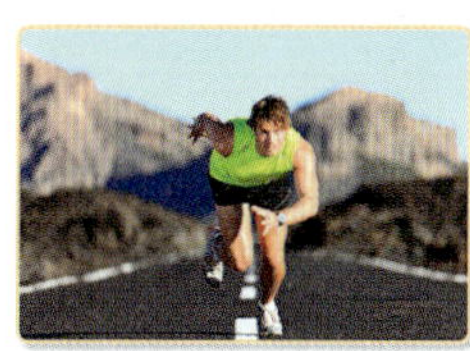

He runs fast ______________ a horse.

그는 말처럼 빨리 달린다.

A 우리말과 같은 뜻이 되도록 보기 에서 알맞은 전치사를 골라 쓰세요. (중복 사용 가능)

보기	up	down	across	through	from	to
	like	by	with	about	without	

1 He slowly went ______down______ the hill.
그는 천천히 언덕을 내려갔다.

2 It takes ________________ 10 minutes to get to school.
학교까지는 대략 10분 정도 걸린다.

3 The car passed ________________ a tunnel.
그 자동차는 터널을 통과했다.

4 You can't see the movie ________________ crying.
그 영화는 눈물 없이는 볼 수 없다.

5 He walked here ________________ school.
그는 학교에서 여기로 걸어왔다.

6 She goes to work ________________ subway.
그녀는 지하철을 타고 출근한다.

7 We often go ________________ the mountain.
우리는 자주 그 산에 올라간다.

8 I want to go fishing ________________ you.
나는 너와 함께 낚시하러 가고 싶다.

9 She came ________________ the street to see me.
그녀가 도로를 가로질러 나를 보려고 왔다.

10 My brother is very tall, ________________ you.
내 오빠는 너처럼 키가 매우 크다.

11 We go ________________ the library every day.
우리는 매일 도서관에 간다.

12 Why does an apple fall ________________?
사과는 왜 아래로 떨어질까?

B 우리말과 같은 뜻이 되도록 (   ) 안에서 알맞은 것을 고르세요.

1 The man ran away (by / through) the window.
그 남자는 창문을 통해 도망쳤다.

2 The bird climbed (up / with) to the clouds.
그 새는 구름 위로 올라갔다.

3 She told me (about / across) her cat.
그녀는 나에게 자기 고양이에 관해 말했다.

4 He goes to school (by / from) bicycle.
그는 자전거로 등교한다.

5 We can't live (to / without) money.
우리는 돈 없이는 살 수 없다.

6 The man ate lunch (with / like) his sister.
그 남자는 그의 여동생과 점심을 먹었다.

7 A cat is walking (across / through) the grass.
고양이 한 마리가 풀밭을 가로질러 걸어가고 있다.

8 The boy often goes (by / to) the bakery.
그 남자아이는 제과점에 자주 간다.

9 A lot of snow fell (from / through) the sky.
많은 눈이 하늘에서 내렸다.

10 Look at the girl (like / with) blue eyes.
푸른색 눈을 가진 소녀를 보세요.

11 Autumn leaves are falling (down / across).
낙엽들이 아래로 떨어지고 있다.

12 He looked out (across / through) the hole.
그는 구멍을 통해 밖을 내다보았다.

A 우리말과 같은 뜻이 되도록 보기 에서 알맞은 전치사를 골라 쓰세요.

> 보기   with   without   by   like   about
>   up   down   through   from   to

1 The pear was very sweet _______like_______ honey.
그 배는 꿀처럼 매우 달았다.

2 I want to go to the moon _______________ rocket.
나는 로켓을 타고 달에 가고 싶다.

3 Look at that child _______________ big eyes.
커다란 눈을 가진 저 아이를 봐.

4 The basketball player is _______________ two meters tall.
그 농구선수는 키가 대략 2미터이다.

5 We can't live _______________ air.
우리는 공기 없이는 살 수 없다.

6 I went _______________ the museum last Sunday.
나는 지난 일요일에 박물관에 갔다.

7 The bubbles start to go _______________.
비눗방울이 위로 올라가기 시작한다.

8 We had to go _______________ the forest.
우리는 숲을 통과해야 했다.

9 A tiger came _______________ from the mountain.
호랑이가 산에서 내려왔다.

10 This bus runs _______________ Daejeon to Changwon.
이 버스는 대전에서 창원까지 운행된다.

B 사진을 보고 우리말과 같은 뜻이 되도록 빈칸에 알맞은 전치사를 쓰세요.

1　They are climbing _______up_______ the mountain.
그들은 산을 올라가고 있는 중이다.

2　She runs very fast _______________ a deer.
그녀는 사슴처럼 매우 빨리 달린다.

3　She likes traveling _______________ train.
그녀는 기차 여행을 좋아한다.

4　He is coming _______________ the hill.
그는 언덕을 내려오고 있다.

5　A horse ran _______________ the field.
말 한 마리가 들판을 가로질러 달렸다.

6　She slept for _______________ two hours.
그녀는 대략 두 시간 동안 잤다.

A 우리말과 같은 뜻이 되도록 주어진 말을 바르게 배열하세요.

1 비행기가 하늘을 날고 있다. (the sky / in / flying up)

→ The plane is 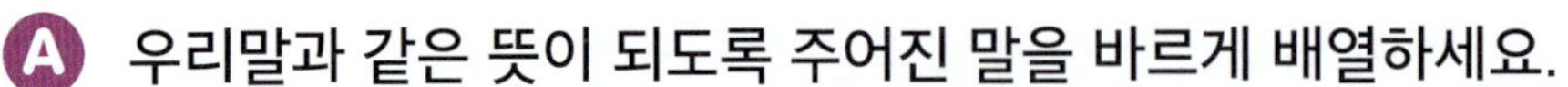 _______ flying up in the sky _______.

2 나는 오늘 내 친구와 함께 수학을 공부할 것이다. (my friend / with / math / study)

→ I will _______________________ today.

3 나는 집에서 학교까지 버스로 간다. (from / school / my house)

→ I go to _______________________ by bus.

4 나는 어제 빨간 머리를 한 소녀를 보았다. (red hair / a girl / with)

→ I saw _______________________ yesterday.

5 그 공주는 천사처럼 웃는다. (an angel / smiles / like)

→ The princess _______________________.

6 자동차들이 터널을 통과하고 있다. (through / going / the tunnel)

→ The cars are _______________________.

7 나는 버스 여행을 매우 좋아한다. (bus / like / by / traveling)

→ I _______________________ very much.

8 곰 한 마리가 언덕을 달려 내려오고 있었다. (down / the hill / running)

→ A bear was _______________________.

9 그녀는 꽃들에 관한 시를 썼다. (about / a poem / flowers)

→ She wrote _______________________.

10 나 없이 쇼핑하러 가지 마. (without / shopping / me / go)

→ Don't _______________________.

B 우리말과 같은 뜻이 되도록 주어진 단어를 이용하여 문장을 완성하세요.

1 내 삼촌은 배를 타고 그 섬에 갔다. (island, ship)

→ My uncle went to ______the island by ship______.

2 그녀는 호수를 가로질러 헤엄치고 있다. (swim, the lake)

→ She is ________________________.

3 기차가 터널을 통과하고 있다. (go, the tunnel)

→ The train is ________________________.

4 어제 우리는 박물관에 걸어서 갔다. (walk, the museum)

→ Yesterday we ________________________.

5 그 남자아이가 계단 아래로 내려오고 있다. (come, the stairs)

→ The boy is ________________________.

6 그는 그의 친구들과 축구를 했다. (play soccer, friends)

→ He ________________________.

7 그는 그녀의 도움 없이 파스타 요리를 했다. (cook, pasta, her help)

→ He ________________________.

8 벌 한 마리가 창문으로 들어왔다. (come in, the window)

→ A bee ________________________.

9 새 한 마리가 하늘 높이 날고 있다. (fly, high)

→ A bird is ________________________ in the sky.

10 그 과일은 호박처럼 생겼다. (look, a pumpkin)

→ The fruit ________________________.

A 우리말과 같은 뜻이 되도록 밑줄 친 부분을 바르게 고쳐 문장을 다시 쓰세요.

1 She had dinner <u>like</u> her family.　그녀는 그녀의 가족과 함께 저녁을 먹었다.

→ _She had dinner with her family._

2 He goes to school <u>with</u> bicycle.　그는 자전거를 타고 학교에 간다.

→ _______________________________________

3 She drove <u>from</u> the village.　그녀는 마을을 통과해서 차를 몰았다.

→ _______________________________________

4 She ran <u>down</u> the road.　그녀는 도로를 가로질러 뛰었다.

→ _______________________________________

5 She is reading a book <u>by</u> Korean history.　그녀는 한국 역사에 관한 책을 읽고 있다.

→ _______________________________________

6 My brother goes to school <u>by</u> foot.　내 남동생은 걸어서 학교에 간다.

→ _______________________________________

7 He is climbing <u>over</u> the ladder.　그는 사다리를 오르고 있다.

→ _______________________________________

8 The ducks are swimming <u>from</u> the pond.　오리들이 연못을 가로질러 헤엄치고 있다.

→ _______________________________________

9 She went out <u>through</u> a mask.　그녀는 마스크 없이 외출했다.

→ _______________________________________

10 The cat fell <u>on</u> the roof.　고양이가 지붕에서 떨어졌다.

→ _______________________________________

B 우리말과 같은 뜻이 되도록 주어진 말을 바르게 배열하세요.

1 나뭇잎이 아래로 떨어지고 있다. (falling / the leaf / down / is / .)

→ The leaf is falling down.

2 그녀는 운동장을 가로질러 달렸다. (the playground / ran / she / across / .)

→ ____

3 나 없이 캠핑하러 가지 마. (without / go / don't / me / camping / .)

→ ____

4 이 캔디는 오렌지 같은 맛이 난다. (an orange / tastes / this candy / like / .)

→ ____

5 모기 한 마리가 구멍을 통해 들어왔다. (came in / a mosquito / the hole / through / .)

→ ____

6 나는 그와 함께 쇼핑을 가고 싶다. (want / I / with / shopping / to / go / him / .)

→ ____

7 그들은 자동차에 관한 이야기를 하고 있다. (cars / are / about / they / talking / .)

→ ____

8 사과 하나가 나무에서 떨어졌다. (from / the tree / fell / an apple / .)

→ ____

9 나비들이 꽃에서 꽃으로 날아다닌다. (from / butterflies / flower / to / flower / fly / .)

→ ____

10 오토바이가 언덕을 올라가고 있다. (the hill / going / is / a motorcycle / up / .)

→ ____

LEVEL UP

 우리말과 같은 뜻이 되도록 빈칸에 알맞은 말을 쓰세요.

1 She came ___________ across ___________ ___________ the ___________
___________ street ___________ to see me.
그녀가 도로를 가로질러 나를 보러 왔다.

2 Sunlight comes in ___________ ___________
___________.
구멍을 통해 햇빛이 들어온다.

3 A starfish looks ___________ ___________
___________.
불가사리는 별처럼 생겼다.

4 Look at the girl ___________ ___________
___________.
금발머리를 가진 소녀를 보세요.

5 An iguana is climbing ___________ ___________
___________.
이구아나가 벽을 올라가고 있다.

6 She goes to work ___________ ___________.
그녀는 지하철을 타고 출근한다.

B 우리말과 같은 뜻이 되도록 빈칸에 알맞은 말을 쓰세요.

1 My family will ____go____ ____to____ ____the____ ____zoo____ .
우리 가족은 동물원에 갈 것이다.

2 He ____________ ____________ ____________ ____________.
그는 광장을 가로질러 달렸다.

3 We can't ____________ ____________ ____________.
우리는 사랑 없이는 살 수 없어.

4 A balloon is coming ____________ ____________ ____________

____________. 풍선이 땅으로 내려오고 있다.

5 She went to London ____________ ____________.
그녀는 비행기를 타고 런던에 갔다.

6 Look at that child ____________ ____________ ____________.
커다란 눈을 가진 저 아이를 봐.

7 Let's talk ____________ ____________ ____________.
너의 꿈에 관해 이야기해 보자.

8 The baby smiles ____________ ____________ ____________.
그 아기는 천사처럼 웃는다.

9 He is ____________ ____________ ____________ ____________.
그는 사다리를 오르고 있다.

10 The train is going ____________ ____________ ____________.
기차가 터널을 통과하고 있다.

[1~3] 우리말을 영어로 바르게 옮긴 것을 고르세요.

1 도서관 옆에 체육관이 있다.
① There is a gym next to the library.
② There is a gym behind the library.

2 사흘 동안 눈이 내렸다.
① It snowed during three days.
② It snowed for three days.

3 오리들이 길을 가로질러 건너고 있다.
① Ducks are walking across the road.
② Ducks are walking between the road.

[4~5] 우리말과 같은 뜻이 되도록 빈칸에 들어갈 알맞은 말을 고르세요.

4 그녀는 아들을 7시까지 기다렸다.
(She waited for her son ______________ 7 o'clock.)

① for   ② by   ③ from   ④ until

5 두 건물 사이에 주차장이 있다.
(There is a parking lot ______________ the two buildings.)

① behind   ② next to   ③ between   ④ in front of

6 빈칸에 들어갈 말이 바르게 짝지어진 것을 고르세요.

> I will go __________ Brazil __________ airplane __________ Wednesday. (나는 수요일에 비행기로 브라질에 갈 것이다.)

① to – by – on
② to – on – in
③ from – by – on
④ for – by – in

[7~8] 빈칸에 공통으로 알맞은 말을 고르세요.

7
> · There are some oranges ______________ the table.
> · I go to the park ______________ Sunday.

① in
② at
③ on
④ by

8
> · The child is ______________ 5 years old.
> · She is writing a book ______________ plants.

① in
② on
③ for
④ about

9 어법상 올바른 문장을 고르세요.

① I was born on 2009.

② My sister gets up in 8 o'clock.

③ We will finish the work by noon.

④ They go jogging at the morning.

10 밑줄 친 부분이 <u>어색한</u> 것을 고르세요.

① He was standing <u>in front of</u> a mirror.

② Many shooting stars are falling <u>down</u>.

③ My father went to London <u>by</u> airplane.

④ She watered the garden <u>for</u> lunchtime.

11 빈칸에 들어갈 말이 바르게 짝지어진 것을 고르세요.

> · I have to finish my homework _____________ Friday.
> · There is a library _____________ the hospital.

① on – between 　　② by – next to

③ in – in front of 　　④ until – during

12 빈칸에 at이 들어갈 수 <u>없는</u> 문장을 고르세요.

① Don't go out _______ night.

② I met my friends _______ noon.

③ He waited for her _______ the bus stop.

④ I visited my grandmother _______ her birthday.

13 우리말을 영어로 바르게 옮긴 것을 고르세요.

> 우리는 공기 없이 살 수 없다.

① We cannot live by air.

② We cannot live for air.

③ We cannot live from air.

④ We cannot live without air.

14 어법상 <u>틀린</u> 부분을 찾아 바르게 고쳐 쓰세요.

> Many cars pass across the tunnel.
> (많은 자동차들이 그 터널을 통과한다.)

_______________________ ➡ _______________________

15 우리말과 같은 뜻이 되도록 주어진 말을 바르게 배열하세요.

> 그 기차는 서울에서 춘천까지 운행한다.
> (Seoul / to / runs / Chuncheon / the train / from / .)

➡ ____

16 그림을 보고 빈칸에 알맞은 전치사를 쓰세요.

There is a bench _____________ the trees.

A dog is sleeping _____________ the bench.

There are two cats _____________ the bench.

A rabbit is _____________ the apple tree.

문장의 형태

Unit 01 주어 + 동사 (+ 주격보어)

Unit 02 주어 + 동사 + 목적어

Unit 03 주어 + 동사 + 목적어 + 목적어

Unit 04 주어 + 동사 + 목적어 + 목적격 보어

학습목표

1 「주어 + 동사」나 「주어 + 동사 + 보어」 형태의 문장에 대해 알아보아요.
2 「주어 + 동사 + 목적어」 형태의 문장에 대해 알아보아요.
3 동사 뒤에 두 개의 목적어가 오는 문장에 대해 알아보아요.
4 동사 뒤에 목적어와 보어가 오는 문장에 대해 알아보아요.

WORD CHECK

neighbor
이웃

cinema
영화관

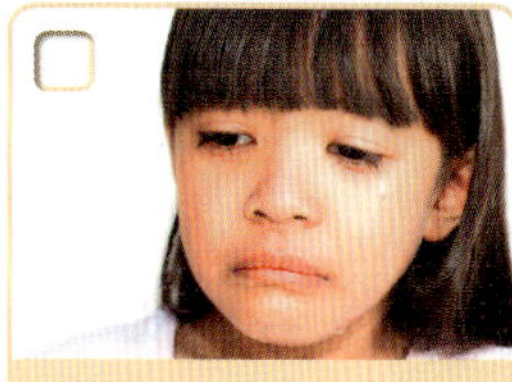
weep
울다

bark
짖다

windy
바람이 많이 부는

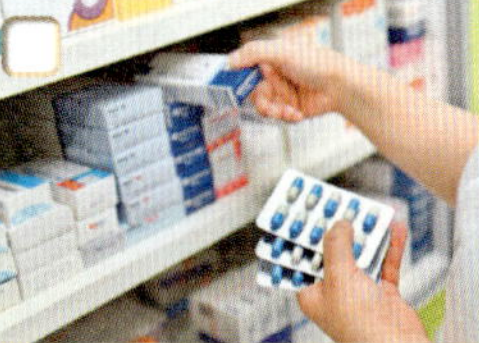
medicine
약, 약물

bowl
그릇

silent
조용한

successful
성공한

airport
공항

send
보내다

elect
뽑다, 선출하다

garlic
마늘

wet
젖은

fear
두려움, 공포

chairman
의장

offer
제안하다

upset
속상한

spinach
시금치

nail
손톱

주어 + 동사 (+ 주격보어)

● 영어의 문장은 5가지 형태로 나눌 수 있어요. 그중에 「주어 + 동사」로 이루어진 문장을 1형식이라고 해요.

주어	동사
Jane	**smiled**. Jane은 미소를 지었다.
I	**am reading**. 나는 책을 읽고 있다.

My friend **arrived**. 내 친구가 도착했다.

I **don't know**. 나는 모른다.

> **Tip** 주어, 동사 다음에 부사(구)를 넣어 '어떻게, 언제, 어디서' 그 동작이 이루어졌는지를 표현할 수 있어요. 동사를 꾸며주는 어구이므로 부사구라고 해요.
> Jane smiled **beautifully**. Jane은 아름답게 웃었다.
> He arrived **at that moment**. 그는 그 순간에 도착했다.

● 「주어 + 동사 + 보어」로 이루어진 문장을 2형식이라고 해요. 보어로는 형용사나 명사가 올 수 있으며, 주어를 보충해주는 말이므로 주격보어라고 해요.

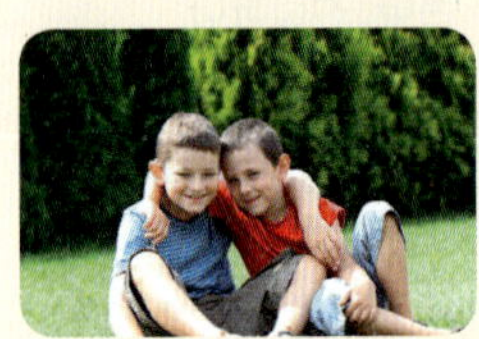

They are **young**. 그들은 어리다.

They are **cute**. 그들은 귀엽다.

They are **my friends**. 그들은 내 친구들이다.

● 다음 동사들 뒤에 형용사가 보어로 올 수 있어요.

주어	+	look 보이다 smell 냄새가 나다 feel 느낌이 들다	sound 들리다 taste 맛이 나다 seem ~인 것 같다	+	보어 (형용사)

The puppy **looks beautiful**. 그 강아지는 아름다워 보인다.

It **sounds good**. 그거 좋은 생각이야.

The steak **smells good**. 스테이크가 맛있는 냄새가 난다.

The cake **tastes sweet**. 케이크 맛이 달다.

His new neighbors **seem nice**. 그의 새 이웃들은 좋아 보인다.

CHECK UP

A 「주어 + 동사」로 된 문장은 1, 「주어 + 동사 + 보어」로 된 문장은 2를 쓰세요.

1 The bus is coming.
버스가 오고 있다.

`1`

2 Cathy is tall.
Cathy는 키가 크다.

3 The students are waiting.
학생들이 기다리고 있다.

4 She became a doctor.
그녀는 의사가 되었다.

5 He seems nice.
그는 멋져 보인다.

6 He is working.
그는 일하고 있다.

B 사진을 보고 빈칸에 들어갈 말로 알맞은 것을 고르세요.

1 
ⓐ sleepy
ⓑ sleep

You look ___________.
너는 졸려 보인다.

2 
ⓐ goodness
ⓑ good

Dinner smells ___________.
저녁 식사가 맛있는 냄새가 난다.

3 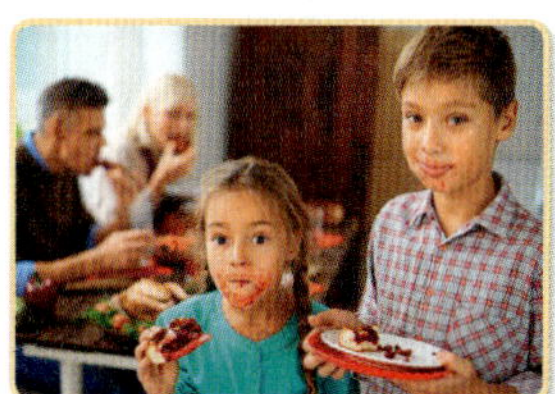
ⓐ great
ⓑ greatly

The pie tastes ___________.
파이가 맛이 좋다.

4
ⓐ beautifully
ⓑ beautiful

That dress looks ___________.
저 드레스는 아름다워 보인다.

주어 + 동사 + 목적어

- 「주어 + 동사 + 목적어」로 이루어진 문장을 3형식이라고 해요. 목적어로는 명사나 대명사가 올 수 있으며, '(무엇)을' '(누구)를'이라는 뜻이에요.

주어	동사	목적어 (~을, ~를)
My friends	like	me. (대명사) 내 친구들은 나를 좋아한다.
She	has	a cellphone. (명사) 그녀는 휴대전화가 있다.

He is wearing **a cap**.   그는 모자를 쓰고 있다.

They didn't do **that**.   그들은 그것을 하지 않았다.

I made a **mistake**.   나는 실수를 했다.

- 목적어 다음에 장소나 시간 등을 나타내는 말이 이어질 수 있어요.

주어	동사	목적어	장소	시간
We 우리는	are going to meet 만나려고 한다	our friends 친구들을	outside the cinema 영화관 밖에서	at 7:30. 7시 30분에.
The man 그 남자는	cleared 청소했다	the snow 눈을	from the streets 거리의	this morning. 오늘 아침에.

- 타동사인 like, build, visit, take, leave, say 등은 목적어를 필요로 하지만, 어떤 타동사는 의미가 확실한 경우 목적어 없이 쓸 수도 있어요.

A: Where is the boy?   그 소년은 어디 있니?

B: He just **left**.   그는 (집을) 막 떠났다.

A: What is Mina doing?   미나는 무엇을 하고 있니?

B: She is **reading**.   그녀는 (책을) 읽고 있어.

Don't talk to Tom now. He is **writing**.   Tom에게 말 걸지 마라. 그는 (글을) 쓰고 있다.

> **Tip** 목적어는 주어와 다른 사물이나 사람을 나타내며, 주어와 목적어의 위치를 바꾸면 문장의 의미도 바뀌어요.
> **The boy** hit **the ball**. 소년이 공을 쳤다.
> **The ball** hit **the boy**. 그 공이 소년을 맞혔다. (그 공에 소년이 맞았다.)

정답 및 해설 p.9

A 다음 문장에서 목적어를 찾아 밑줄을 그으세요.

1 We baked <u>some cookies</u>.   우리는 과자를 좀 구웠다.

2 The company makes computers.   그 회사는 컴퓨터를 만든다.

3 He posted a message on a website.   그는 웹사이트에 메시지를 올렸다.

4 She was eating a sandwich.   그녀는 샌드위치를 먹고 있었다.

5 She likes comic books very much.   그녀는 만화책을 무척 좋아한다.

6 I bought a new cap yesterday.   나는 어제 새 모자를 샀다.

B 사진을 보고 알맞은 말에 V 표시하세요.

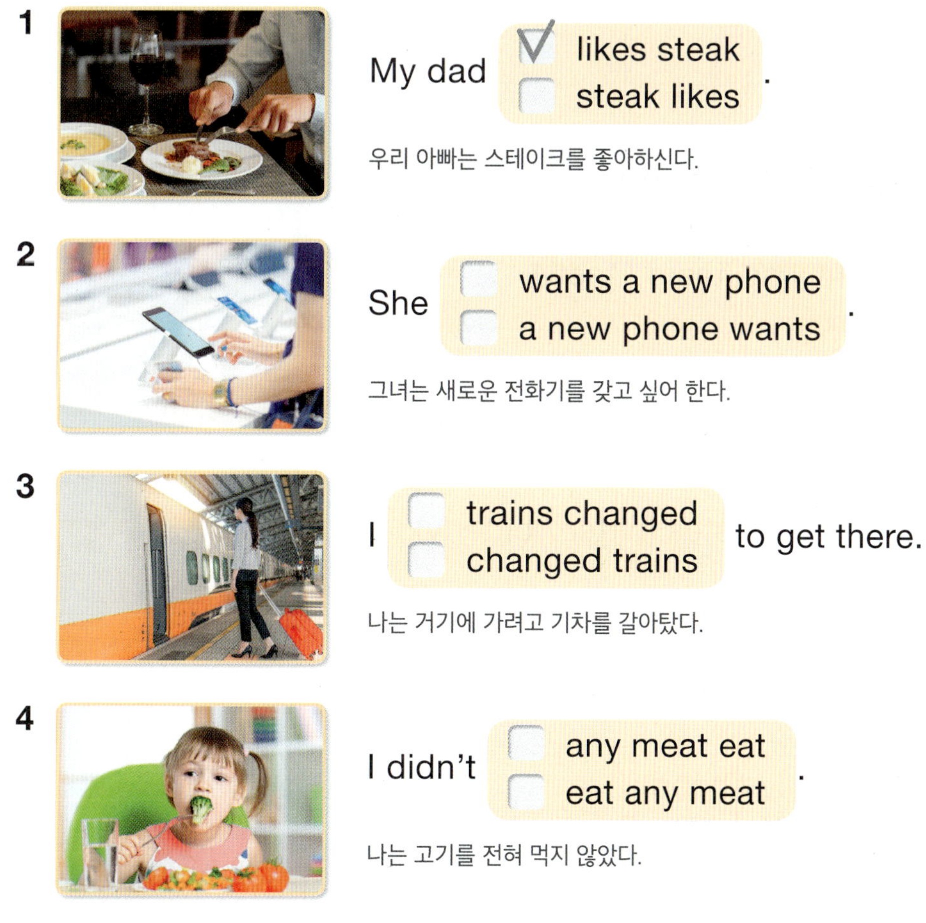

1 My dad ☑ likes steak / ☐ steak likes .

우리 아빠는 스테이크를 좋아하신다.

2 She ☐ wants a new phone / ☐ a new phone wants .

그녀는 새로운 전화기를 갖고 싶어 한다.

3 I ☐ trains changed / ☐ changed trains to get there.

나는 거기에 가려고 기차를 갈아탔다.

4 I didn't ☐ any meat eat / ☐ eat any meat .

나는 고기를 전혀 먹지 않았다.

「주어 + 동사」나「주어 + 동사 + 보어」형태를 연습해 봐요.

A 밑줄 친 부분이 맞으면 ○, 틀리면 X 표시하세요.

1 The bell rang.
벨이 울렸다.
→ O

2 My little sister wept.
내 여동생은 울었다.
→

3 Jack is busily these days.
Jack은 요즘 바쁘다.
→

4 She was sick.
그녀는 아팠다.
→

5 The dog barked loudly.
그 개는 큰 소리로 짖었다.
→

6 The bus came lately.
버스가 늦게 왔다.
→

B ( ) 안에서 알맞은 것을 고르세요.

1 The ice cream was (taste / tasty).
아이스크림은 맛있었다.

2 It was (windy / wind) last night.
어젯밤에는 바람이 불었다.

3 A good medicine tastes (bitter / bitterly).
좋은 약은 입에 쓰다.

4 These dancers jump (good / well).
이 무용수들은 점프를 잘한다.

5 They feel (happily / happy).
그들은 행복하다고 느낀다.

정답 및 해설 p.9

A 주어진 단어가 들어갈 위치를 고르세요.

1 Mom loves ⓐ and ⓑ my brother. (me)
엄마는 나와 내 남동생을 사랑하신다.

2 I ordered ⓐ for ⓑ lunch. (a pizza)
나는 점심으로 피자를 주문했다.

3 Cathy eats ⓐ a day ⓑ. (two bowls of salad)
Cathy는 하루에 두 그릇의 샐러드를 먹는다.

4 Do you ⓐ ride ⓑ on Sundays? (your bike)
너는 일요일마다 자전거를 타니?

5 I'm going to meet ⓐ in the library ⓑ at 9:30. (my friends)
나는 9시 30분에 내 친구들을 도서관에서 만날 것이다.

B 다음 문장에서 목적어를 찾아 쓰세요.

1 Ted and Jane do their homework every day. → <u>their homework</u>
Ted와 Jane은 매일 그들의 숙제를 한다.

2 My brother helps me a lot. → ______________
우리 형은 나를 많이 도와준다.

3 Firefighters use masks and ropes. → ______________
소방관들은 마스크와 밧줄을 사용한다.

4 She usually puts some cheese on her hamburger. → ______________
그녀는 보통 햄버거에 치즈를 좀 올린다.

5 Does the girl need more time? → ______________
그 소녀는 시간이 더 필요하니?

6 Add two slices of ham. → ______________
두 장의 햄을 더 얹어라.

A 다음 문장에서 보어나 목적어에 밑줄을 긋고, 보어면 C, 목적어면 O를 쓰세요.

1 I really miss <u>my friends</u>.
나는 내 친구들이 정말 그립다.

O

2 The book becomes interesting in Chapter 2.
그 책은 두 번째 챕터부터 흥미로워진다.

3 Many students study Korean history.
많은 학생들이 한국 역사를 공부한다.

4 Do you sometimes feel lonely?
너는 가끔 외롭다고 느끼니?

5 My dad reads newspapers every morning.
우리 아빠는 매일 아침 신문을 읽으신다.

6 You look happy today.
너는 오늘 행복해 보이는구나.

7 Bakers make bread and cakes.
제빵사들은 빵과 케이크를 만든다.

8 I borrowed his book yesterday.
나는 그의 책을 어제 빌렸다.

9 The sky turned dark after lunch.
하늘이 점심 이후에 어둡게 변했다.

10 The young singer became famous.
그 젊은 가수는 유명해졌다.

11 Cathy practices piano two hours a day.
Cathy는 피아노를 하루에 두 시간씩 연습한다.

12 My classmates study English very hard.
우리 반 친구들은 영어를 열심히 공부한다.

B 우리말과 같은 뜻이 되도록 보기 에서 알맞은 말을 골라 쓰세요.

> 보기 buy clothes   love music   teaches math   become rich
> sounds great   kept silent   gets angry   feels sad
> walk to school   looks cold

1 The weather today _____________ looks cold _____________.
오늘 날씨는 추워 보인다.

2 Everyone _____________________________ at times.
모든 사람은 때로 슬프다고 느낀다.

3 That person _____________________________ very easily.
그 사람은 매우 쉽게 화를 낸다.

4 We all want to _____________________________, right?
우리 모두는 부자가 되길 원해, 그렇지?

5 A: Do you want to go to the movies and eat burgers?
영화관에 가서 햄버거를 먹고 싶니?
B: Yeah, that _____________________________!
응, 정말 좋은 생각이야!

6 She _____________________________ at a middle school.
그녀는 중학교에서 수학을 가르친다.

7 The children _____________________________.
그 아이들은 걸어서 학교에 간다.

8 Where can I _____________________________ right now?
지금 당장 어디서 옷을 살 수 있니?

9 Why do we _____________________________?
우리는 왜 음악을 사랑할까?

10 She _____________________________ during the meeting.
그녀는 회의를 하는 동안 잠자코 있었다.

STEP UP 2

A 우리말과 같은 뜻이 되도록 주어진 말을 이용하여 문장을 완성하세요.

1 I ___________ wear glasses ___________ for reading. (glasses, wear)
나는 책을 읽을 때 안경을 쓴다.

2 I'll ___________ outside the theater at 8:00. (him, meet)
8시에 극장 밖에서 그를 만날 거야.

3 It's Kelly's turn to ___________. (the table, clear)
Kelly가 테이블을 치울 차례이다.

4 She ___________ hard. (hit, him)
그녀는 그를 세게 때렸다.

5 I will ___________ so much. (miss, her)
나는 그녀가 정말 그리울 거야.

6 I'm ___________ for Alex. (a cake, bake)
나는 Alex를 위해 케이크를 굽고 있어.

7 That company ___________. (dresses, make)
저 회사는 드레스를 만든다.

8 He ___________ on a website. (a notice, post)
그는 한 웹사이트에 게시물을 올렸다.

9 The girl was ___________. (eat, an ice cream)
그 소녀는 아이스크림을 먹고 있었다.

10 Do you ___________? (this color, like)
너는 이 색깔을 좋아하니?

11 I ___________ yesterday. (a new dress, buy)
나는 어제 새 드레스를 샀다.

12 He ___________. (a new car, want)
그는 새로운 차를 원한다.

B 사진을 보고 우리말과 같은 뜻이 되도록 주어진 말을 이용하여 문장을 완성하세요.

1 The train _______ is _______ _______ coming _______.
(come)
기차가 오고 있다.

2 _______________ _______________ at me.
(she, smile)
그녀는 내게 미소를 지었다.

3 The puppy _______________ _______________.
(cute, look)
그 강아지는 귀여워 보인다.

4 The steak _______________ _______________.
(delicious, smell)
그 스테이크는 맛있는 냄새가 난다.

5 _______________ _______________ at the office.
(arrive, she)
그녀는 사무실에 도착했다.

6 Mm! This _______________ _______________!
(good, taste)
음! 이건 정말 맛이 좋은데!

A 우리말과 같은 뜻이 되도록 주어진 말을 바르게 배열하세요.

1 그 무용수들은 키가 컸다. (dancers / tall / were)

→ The _______ dancers were tall _______.

2 그는 55세의 나이에 대통령이 되었다. (president / he / became)

→ ________________________________ at the age of 55.

3 그녀는 아주 완벽해 보인다. (looks / perfect / so)

→ She ________________________________.

4 음! 이 꽃은 좋은 향기가 나는데! (smells / this flower / good)

→ Mm! ________________________________!

5 그 음식은 보기보다 맛이 좋았다. (the food / better / tasted)

→ ________________________________ than it looked.

6 저 드레스는 상당히 안 좋아 보인다. (pretty / looks / bad)

→ That dress ________________________________.

7 누구 좋은 생각 없나요? (a / idea / good / have)

→ Does anybody ________________________________?

8 그는 야구를 좋아하지만 축구는 정말 좋아한다. (soccer / loves / he)

→ He likes baseball, but ________________________________.

9 그는 생일 선물로 자전거를 원한다. (a / bicycle / wants / he)

→ ________________________________ for his birthday.

10 그는 거기에 가려고 비행기를 갈아탔다. (planes / changed / he)

→ ________________________________ to get there.

B 우리말과 같은 뜻이 되도록 밑줄 친 부분을 바르게 고쳐 문장을 다시 쓰세요.

1 Rang the phone loudly. 전화벨이 큰 소리로 울렸다.

→ The phone rang loudly.

2 He weeping for joy. 그는 기쁨의 눈물을 흘렸다.

→

3 Farmers are very busily these days. 농부들은 요즘 매우 바쁘다.

→

4 She is sickness with the flu. 그녀는 독감으로 아프다.

→

5 The big dog was barked. 그 큰 개는 짖고 있었다.

→

6 The train is a half hour lately. 그 기차는 30분 늦었다.

→

7 I ordered to the books from a website. 나는 웹사이트에서 책들을 주문했다.

→

8 Do you ride to your motorcycle every day? 너는 오토바이를 매일 타니?

→

9 She studied hardly to pass the exam. 그녀는 시험에 합격하기 위해 열심히 공부했다.

→

10 Add to a little more salt and pepper. 소금과 후추를 조금 더 넣어라.

→

STEP UP 4

 우리말과 같은 뜻이 되도록 주어진 말을 이용하여 문장을 완성하세요.

1 어제는 더웠다. (it, yesterday, hot)

➡ _______________ It was hot yesterday.

2 음식은 맛있고 신선했다. (the food, tasty, fresh, and)

➡ _______________________________________

3 이 약은 맛이 쓰다. (this medicine, bitter, tastes)

➡ _______________________________________

4 그들은 한국 문화를 공부한다. (culture, Korean, study)

➡ _______________________________________

5 너는 지금 기분이 나아졌니? (feel, do, now, better)

➡ _______________________________________

6 내 고양이는 점프를 잘 못한다. (my cat, jump, well, can't)

➡ _______________________________________

7 나는 그의 펜을 빌렸다. (his, borrowed, pen)

➡ _______________________________________

8 그들은 토요일에 축구 연습을 한다. (soccer, practice, Saturday, on)

➡ _______________________________________

9 그 가수는 성공하게 되었다. (the singer, became, successful)

➡ _______________________________________

10 하늘이 점심 이후에 빨갛게 변했다. (the sky, red, turned, after, lunch)

➡ _______________________________________

B 어법상 <u>틀린</u> 부분을 찾아 문장을 다시 쓰세요.

1 The man ran quick to the building.   그 남자는 재빨리 건물로 달려갔다.

→ The man ran quickly to the building.

2 She looks happily today.   그녀는 오늘 행복해 보인다.

→

3 She English studies on Mondays.   그녀는 월요일마다 영어를 공부한다.

→

4 Firefighters use equipment heavy.   소방관들은 무거운 장비를 사용한다.

→

5 They didn't do this correct.   그들은 이것을 올바르게 하지 못했다.

→

6 I met at the airport my friend.   나는 공항에서 내 친구를 만났다.

→

7 A man cleared outside a house the snow.   한 남자가 집 밖의 눈을 치웠다.

→

8 We walk school to every day.   우리는 매일 걸어서 학교에 간다.

→

9 She kept silently during the discussion.   그녀는 토론하는 동안 침묵을 지켰다.

→

10 I made on the test a mistake.   나는 시험에서 실수를 했다.

→

A 우리말과 같은 뜻이 되도록 빈칸에 알맞은 말을 쓰세요.

1

She ________became________ ________a________ ________doctor________.

그녀는 의사가 되었다.

2

The bus ________________ ________________.

버스가 늦게 왔다.

3

Mom ________________ ________________ and my ________________.

엄마는 나와 내 남동생을 사랑하신다.

4

Do you ________________ ________________ ________________ on Sundays?

너는 일요일마다 네 자전거를 타니?

5

I ________________ ________________ ________________ for lunch.

나는 점심으로 피자를 주문했다.

6

The young singer ________________ ________________.

그 젊은 가수는 유명해졌다.

B 우리말과 같은 뜻이 되도록 빈칸에 알맞은 말을 쓰세요.

1 Jack _______is_______ _______busy_______ these days.
Jack은 요즘 바쁘다.

2 _______________ _______________ _______________ last night.
어젯밤에는 바람이 불었다.

3 Many students _______________ _______________ _______________.
많은 학생들이 한국 역사를 공부한다.

4 I _______________ _______________ _______________ yesterday.
나는 어제 그의 책을 빌렸다.

5 The bus _______________ _______________.
버스가 오고 있다.

6 The dog _______________ _______________.
그 개는 큰 소리로 짖었다.

7 He _______________ _______________.
그는 멋져 보인다.

8 I _______________ _______________ to get there.
나는 거기에 가려고 기차를 갈아탔다.

9 That dress _______________ _______________.
저 드레스는 아름다워 보인다.

10 Ted and Jane _______________ _______________ _______________
every day.
Ted와 Jane은 매일 그들의 숙제를 한다.

주어 + 동사 + 목적어 + 목적어

● 어떤 동사들 뒤에는 두 개의 목적어가 쓰이는데, 주로 '(누구에게 무엇을) 해주다'라는 뜻의 동사들이에요. 이러한 형태의 문장을 4형식이라고 해요.

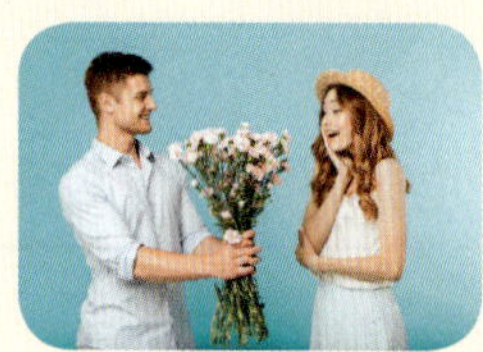

Tony gave **Cathy some flowers**.　Tony는 Cathy에게 꽃을 좀 주었다.
Tony bought **her some flowers**.　Tony는 그녀에게 꽃을 좀 사 주었다.

● '누구에게 무엇을 해주다'라는 형태로 두 개의 목적어를 취하는 동사에는 다음과 같은 것들이 있어요. 이때 사람을 가리키는 목적어가 먼저 오는 경우가 많아요.

| give | show | send | write | buy | tell | lend | pass |

주어	동사	목적어(사람)	목적어(사물)
We	bought	the children	some books. 우리는 그 아이들에게 책을 좀 사주었다.
Tom	sent	Sally	some flowers. Tom은 Sally에게 꽃을 좀 보냈다.
Jane	showed	him	her new phone. Jane은 그에게 자신의 새로운 전화기를 보여 주었다.
Mary	told	the students	a story. Mary는 학생들에게 이야기를 해주었다.

She **gave** me some money. 그녀는 나에게 돈을 좀 주었다.
I **wrote** him a letter. 나는 그에게 편지를 썼다.
Mom **made** me pizza. 엄마는 나에게 피자를 만들어 주셨다.
The man **taught** her English. 그 남자가 그녀에게 영어를 가르쳐 주었다.

> **Tip**　사물을 가리키는 목적어를 먼저 쓰기도 하는데, 이때는 for나 to가 필요해요.
>
> We bought some books **for** the children.　우리는 그 아이들을 위해 몇 권의 책을 샀다.
> Tom sent some flowers **to** Sally.　Tom는 Sally에게 약간의 꽃들을 보냈다.
> Jane showed her new phone **to** him.　Jane은 그에게 그녀의 새 휴대전화를 보여줬다.
> Mary told a story **to** the students.　Mary는 학생들에게 이야기를 들려줬다.

CHECK UP

A 주어진 단어가 들어갈 위치를 고르세요.

1 | me | give ⓐ some money ⓑ   나에게 돈을 좀 주다

2 | her | show ⓐ my pictures ⓑ   그녀에게 내 사진들을 보여주다

3 | an email | send ⓐ him ⓑ   그에게 이메일을 보내다

4 | cookies | make ⓐ us ⓑ   우리에게 과자를 만들어주다

5 | her | ask ⓐ a question ⓑ   그녀에게 질문을 하다

B 사진을 보고 알맞은 말에 V 표시하세요.

1 My friend gave ☑ me / ☐ to me a present.

내 친구가 나에게 선물을 주었다.

2 My brother told ☐ me / ☐ to me his plans.

우리 형은 자신의 계획을 내게 말했다.

3 Cathy will make ☐ a cake you / ☐ you a cake .

Cathy가 네게 케이크를 만들어 줄 것이다.

4 The teacher taught ☐ us English / ☐ English us .

그 선생님은 우리에게 영어를 가르치셨다.

주어 + 동사 + 목적어 + 목적격 보어

● 목적어가 어떤 상태인지를 설명하기 위해 「주어 + 동사 + 목적어 + 목적격 보어」 형태의 문장을 쓸 수 있어요. 이러한 형태의 문장을 5형식이라고 해요.

Tony finds <u>her new song</u> <u>amazing</u>.
　　　　　　목적어　　　　　목적격 보어
Tony는 그녀의 새 노래가 굉장하다고 생각한다.

The song made <u>him</u> <u>happy</u>.
　　　　　　　목적어　목적격 보어
그 노래는 그를 행복하게 했다.

● 이런 형태로 자주 쓰이는 동사에는 다음과 같은 것들이 있으며, 목적격 보어로는 형용사가 자주 쓰여요.

make	The song <u>makes</u> <u>me</u> <u>happy</u>. 그 노래는 나를 행복하게 한다. 　　　　　make　A　B　　(A를 B하게 만들다)
find	I <u>find</u> <u>John</u> really <u>smart</u>. 나는 John이 매우 똑똑하다고 생각한다. 　find　A　　　　B　　(A가 B하다고 생각하다/여기다)
keep	Jane always <u>keeps</u> <u>her room</u> <u>clean</u>. Jane은 항상 자신의 방을 깨끗하게 유지한다. 　　　　　keep　　A　　　B　　(A를 B하게 유지하다)
call	The teacher <u>called</u> <u>me</u> <u>cute</u>. 그 선생님은 나를 귀엽다고 했다. 　　　　　call　A　B　　(A를 B라고 부르다)

● 목적격 보어로 명사가 올 수도 있으며, '(목적어)는 (목적격 보어)이다', 즉 '목적어 = 목적격 보어'의 관계가 돼요.

They elected him **president of the U.S.** 그들은 그를 미국의 대통령으로 선출했다. (him = president)

Don't call me **a liar**. 나를 거짓말쟁이라고 부르지 마. (me = liar)

> **Tip** 부사는 목적격 보어가 될 수 없어요.
> The garlic made the soup **awfully**. (X)
> The garlic made the soup **awful**. (O) 마늘은 수프를 아주 맛없게 만들었다.

CHECK UP

A 주어진 단어가 들어갈 위치를 고르세요.

1 | me | make ⓐ sad ⓑ   나를 슬프게 하다

2 | her | find ⓐ very kind ⓑ   그녀가 매우 친절한 것을 알게 되다

3 | clean | keep ⓐ his room ⓑ   그의 방을 깨끗하게 유지하다

4 | green | paint ⓐ the wall ⓑ   벽을 녹색으로 칠하다

5 | open | leave ⓐ the door ⓑ   문을 열어 두다

B 사진을 보고 알맞은 말에 V 표시하세요.

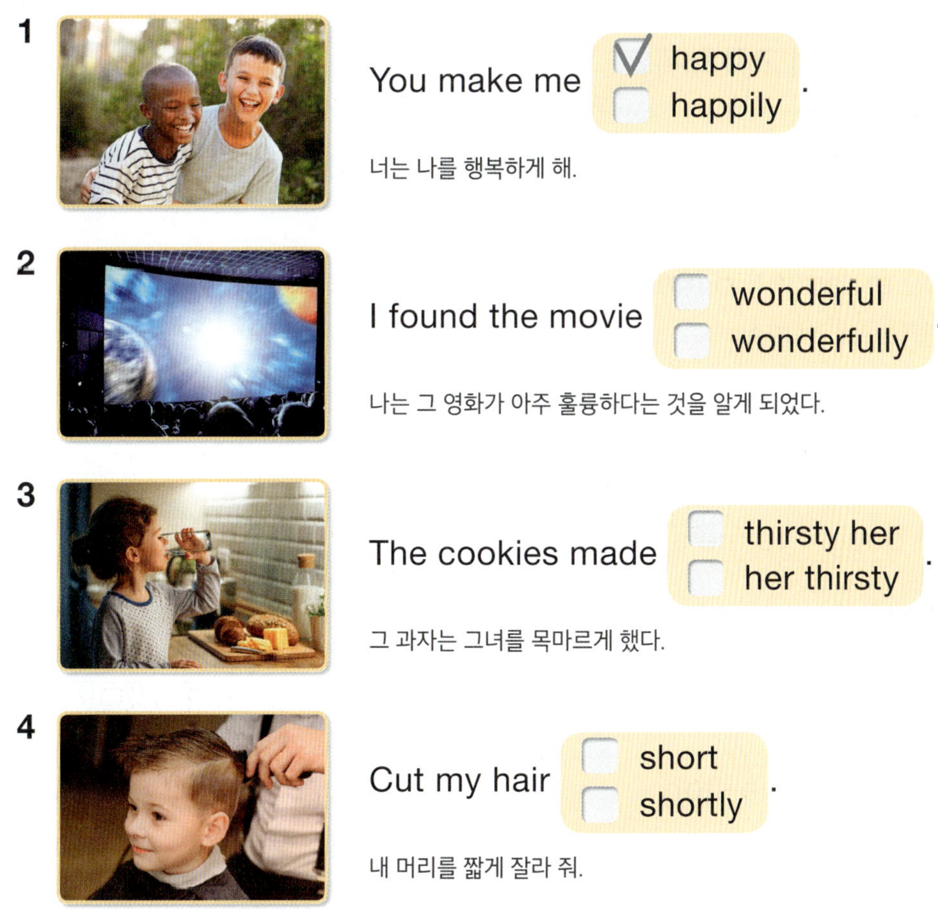

1 You make me ☑ happy / ☐ happily .

너는 나를 행복하게 해.

2 I found the movie ☐ wonderful / ☐ wonderfully .

나는 그 영화가 아주 훌륭하다는 것을 알게 되었다.

3 The cookies made ☐ thirsty her / ☐ her thirsty .

그 과자는 그녀를 목마르게 했다.

4 Cut my hair ☐ short / ☐ shortly .

내 머리를 짧게 잘라 줘.

목적어가 두 개인 표현에 대해 알아 봐요.

A 우리말과 일치하는 문장을 고르세요.

1 나는 그에게 이메일을 보냈다.
   ⓐ I sent him an email.
   ⓑ I sent an email him.

2 Jane은 나에게 비밀을 말했다.
   ⓐ Jane told me a secret.
   ⓑ Jane told a secret me.

3 그는 나에게 모자를 사 주었다.
   ⓐ He bought a cap me.
   ⓑ He bought me a cap.

4 엄마는 내 여동생에게 스웨터를 만들어주셨다.
   ⓐ Mom made a sweater my sister.
   ⓑ Mom made my sister a sweater.

5 그녀는 내게 영어책을 주었다.
   ⓐ She gave me an English book.
   ⓑ She gave an English book me.

B 밑줄 친 부분을 바르게 고쳐 쓰세요.

1 Mary showed to him her pictures. → ____showed him____
   Mary는 그에게 자신의 사진들을 보여주었다.

2 My brother taught to me English. → ________________
   내 형은 나에게 영어를 가르쳐주었다.

3 Jim sent for his friend a gift. → ________________
   Jim은 그의 친구에게 선물을 보냈다.

4 My dad bought to me a bike. → ________________
   아빠는 내게 자전거를 사 주셨다.

5 Mom made for me a pretty doll. → ________________
   엄마는 내게 예쁜 인형을 만들어주셨다.

6 I will tell to you the story. → ________________
   내가 너에게 이야기를 해줄게.

정답 및 해설 p.10

A 다음 문장에서 목적격 보어를 찾아 ○ 표시하세요.

1 The rain made all of us (wet).
비가 우리 모두를 젖게 했다.

2 The box keeps vegetables fresh for longer.
그 상자는 야채를 더 오랫동안 신선하게 보관한다.

3 Homework often makes me tired.
숙제는 종종 나를 지치게 한다.

4 A lot of women find him attractive.
많은 여성들은 그를 매력적이라고 생각한다.

5 She found the work boring.
그녀는 그 일이 따분하다고 느꼈다.

B ( ) 안에서 알맞은 것을 고르세요.

1 She called her friend (a liar / lie).
그녀는 자기 친구를 거짓말쟁이라고 불렀다.

2 The news made her (sadness / sad).
그 소식은 그녀를 슬프게 했다.

3 Fear kept them (quiet / quietly).
공포가 그들을 조용하게 했다.

4 The judge found him (guilt / guilty).
판사는 그를 유죄로 판결했다.

5 Time proved them (right / wrong).
시간이 지나서 그들이 틀렸다는 것이 밝혀졌다.

6 His complaints drive me (craze / crazy).
그의 불평은 나를 미치게 한다.

STEP UP 1

A 우리말과 같은 뜻이 되도록 보기에서 알맞은 말을 골라 쓰세요.

> **보기** bought   elected   makes   named   paint   painted
> sent   show   showed   tell   send

1 She _______bought_______ him some neckties for Christmas.
그녀는 그에게 크리스마스 선물로 넥타이를 좀 사 주었다.

2 Harry _______________ her some flowers.
Harry는 그녀에게 꽃을 좀 보냈다.

3 Mike _______________ Sally his new laptop.
Mike는 Sally에게 그의 새 노트북 컴퓨터를 보여주었다.

4 Jane didn't _______________ the students a story.
Jane은 학생들에게 이야기를 해 주지 않았다.

5 Please _______________ him the tickets.
그에게 티켓들을 보내세요.

6 I'll _______________ you my favorite photos.
내가 가장 좋아하는 사진들을 너에게 보여줄게.

7 Chocolate _______________ Mary happy.
초콜릿은 Mary를 행복하게 한다.

8 He _______________ the box purple.
그는 상자를 자주색으로 칠했다.

9 They _______________ Mike chairman.
그들은 Mike를 의장으로 선출했다.

10 They _______________ their son John.
그들은 그들의 아들 이름을 John이라고 지었다.

11 I want to _______________ my walls blue.
나는 내 벽을 파란색으로 칠하고 싶다.

B 주어진 말이 들어갈 위치를 고르세요.

1 an email

I will send ⓐ the hotel ⓑ to check the prices.
나는 가격을 확인하기 위해 호텔에 메일을 보낼 것이다.

2 the money

Can you pay ⓐ her ⓑ?
당신은 그녀에게 그 돈을 지불할 수 있나요?

3 him

I didn't show ⓐ the photos ⓑ.
나는 그에게 그 사진들을 보여주지 않았다.

4 the students

Cathy teaches ⓐ English novels ⓑ.
Cathy는 그 학생들에게 영국 소설을 가르친다.

5 the job

They offered ⓐ Alex ⓑ.
그들은 Alex에게 그 일자리를 제안했다.

6 a story

Mary told ⓐ the children ⓑ.
Mary는 그 아이들에게 이야기를 하나 해주었다.

7 awful

The garlic made ⓐ the soup ⓑ.
그 마늘이 수프를 아주 맛없게 만들었다.

8 me

Please call ⓐ Jackie ⓑ.
나를 Jackie라고 불러주세요.

9 upset

He made ⓐ Neil ⓑ.
그는 Neil을 화나게 했다.

10 the man

He called ⓐ a liar ⓑ.
그는 그 남자를 거짓말쟁이라고 불렀다.

11 nervous

Public speaking makes ⓐ Henry ⓑ.
대중들 앞에서 말하는 것은 Henry를 불안하게 한다.

A 우리말과 같은 뜻이 되도록 주어진 말을 이용하여 문장을 완성하세요.

1 Can I ask ______you______ ___something___? (something)
너에게 뭐 좀 물어봐도 되니?

2 My brother told ____________ ____________. (that)
우리 형이 그것을 내게 말했다.

3 Cathy will make ____________ ____________ ____________. (a steak)
Cathy가 너에게 스테이크를 만들어 줄 것이다.

4 She taught ____________ ____________. (science)
그녀는 우리에게 과학을 가르치셨다.

5 Sally sent ____________ ____________ ____________. (some, flowers)
Sally는 그에게 꽃을 좀 보냈다.

6 She bought ____________ ____________ ____________ for Christmas.
(a bike)
그녀는 그에게 크리스마스 선물로 자전거를 사 주었다.

7 Singing makes ____________ ____________. (happy)
노래 부르기는 그녀를 행복하게 한다.

8 He painted ____________ ____________ ____________. (the wall, yellow)
그는 그 벽을 노란색으로 칠했다.

9 They elected ____________ ____________ of their team. (captain, Mike)
그들은 Mike를 팀의 주장으로 뽑았다.

10 Jane named ____________ ____________ ____________. (son, David)
Jane은 그녀의 아들 이름을 David라고 지었다.

11 The spinach made ____________ ____________ ____________.
(nice, the soup)
시금치는 수프를 맛있게 만들었다.

12 Please call ____________ ____________. (Julie)
나를 Julie라고 불러주세요.

B 사진을 보고 우리말과 같은 뜻이 되도록 주어진 말을 이용하여 문장을 완성하세요.

1 Mom gave ______*me*______ ______*a*______

______*present*______. (a present)

엄마가 나에게 선물을 주었다.

2 Tony bought ________________ ________________.

(lunch)

Tony는 내게 점심을 사 주었다.

3 He sent ________________ ________________

________________. (an email)

그는 나에게 이메일을 보냈다.

4 Tony finds ________________ ________________

________________. (useful, this box)

Tony는 이 상자가 쓸모 있다고 여긴다.

5 Music makes ________________ ________________.

(happy)

음악은 나를 행복하게 한다.

6 I like to keep ________________ ________________

________________. (clean, room)

나는 내 방을 깨끗하게 유지하는 걸 좋아한다.

A 우리말과 같은 뜻이 되도록 주어진 말을 바르게 배열하세요.

1 그녀는 나에게 크리스마스 선물로 전화기를 사 주었다. (a phone / me / bought)

→ She ___________ bought me a phone ___________ for Christmas.

2 Harry는 그녀에게 빨간 장미를 보냈다. (a red rose / sent / her)

→ Harry ___________________________________.

3 Mike는 나에게 그의 새 전화기를 보여주었다. (me / showed / his new phone)

→ Mike ___________________________________.

4 Jane은 그에게 진실을 말하지 않았다. (tell / the truth / him)

→ Jane didn't ___________________________________.

5 나는 그에게 메시지를 보냈다. (a message / him / sent)

→ I ___________________________________.

6 내가 새로 산 드레스를 보여줄게. (you / show / my new dress)

→ I'll ___________________________________.

7 내 노래가 그녀를 행복하게 했다. (happy / her / made)

→ My song ___________________________________.

8 그는 상자를 빨갛게 칠했다. (painted / red / the box)

→ He ___________________________________.

9 우리는 그를 의장으로 선출했다. (him / elected / the chairperson)

→ We ___________________________________.

10 그들은 그 개의 이름을 Snoopy라고 지었다. (Snoopy / named / the dog)

→ They ___________________________________.

B 밑줄 친 부분을 바르게 고쳐 문장을 다시 쓰세요.

1 Mom <u>bought to me</u> a backpack. 엄마는 나에게 배낭을 사 주셨다.

→ _________ Mom bought me a backpack. _________

2 He <u>sent to her</u> a sunflower. 그는 그녀에게 해바라기 한 송이를 보냈다.

→ _______________________________________

3 Mike <u>showed for me</u> his new computer. Mike는 나에게 그의 새 컴퓨터를 보여주었다.

→ _______________________________________

4 Jane <u>told for them</u> the news. Jane은 그들에게 그 소식을 말해주었다.

→ _______________________________________

5 I <u>lent to him</u> a car. 나는 그에게 차를 빌려주었다.

→ _______________________________________

6 I'll <u>show to you</u> my painting. 내가 너에게 내 그림을 보여줄게.

→ _______________________________________

7 I don't find her <u>attractively</u>. 나는 그녀가 매력적이라고 생각하지 않는다.

→ _______________________________________

8 The box keeps the food <u>freshly</u>. 그 상자는 음식을 신선하게 보관한다.

→ _______________________________________

9 It makes me <u>nervously</u>. 그것은 나를 불안하게 만든다.

→ _______________________________________

10 The snow makes <u>happy me</u>. 눈은 나를 행복하게 한다.

→ _______________________________________

STEP UP 4

A 우리말과 같은 뜻이 되도록 주어진 말을 이용하여 문장을 완성하세요.

1 그들은 문을 열어 두었다. (the door, open, left)

→ _______________ They left the door open. _______________

2 나는 머리를 짧게 자르고 싶다. (want, to cut, short, my hair)

→ ____

3 그는 그녀에게 반지를 사 주었다. (her, a ring, bought)

→ ____

4 엄마는 내게 샌드위치를 만들어주었다. (a sandwich, Mom, made)

→ ____

5 내가 너에게 진실을 말해줄게. (tell, the truth, will)

→ ____

6 그 소식은 우리를 행복하게 했다. (made, happy, the news)

→ ____

7 쇼핑은 나를 지치게 한다. (makes, tired, shopping)

→ ____

8 그는 그 일이 흥미롭다고 생각했다. (found, interesting, the work)

→ ____

9 그들은 그를 준희라고 불렀다. (called, Junhee, him)

→ ____

10 그들은 그가 틀렸다는 것을 증명했다. (him, wrong, proved)

→ ____

B 어법상 <u>틀린</u> 부분을 찾아 문장을 다시 쓰세요.

1 That sound drives me crazily.   그 소리는 나를 미치게 한다.

→ _________________ That sound drives me crazy. _________________

2 The movie makes me sleepily.   그 영화는 나를 졸리게 한다.

→ ____

3 Susan painted red her nails.   Susan은 자신의 손톱을 빨갛게 칠했다.

→ ____

4 Did you pay he the money?   너는 그에게 그 돈을 지불했니?

→ ____

5 They offered to him a good job.   그들은 그에게 좋은 일자리를 제안했다.

→ ____

6 Write to him a letter.   그에게 편지를 써라.

→ ____

7 I want to ask to him a question now.   나는 그에게 지금 질문을 하고 싶다.

→ ____

8 Tony finds her new book amazingly.   Tony는 그녀의 새 책이 굉장하다고 생각한다.

→ ____

9 Does he keep the room cleanly?   그는 방을 깨끗하게 해 놓니?

→ ____

10 Her friends call she Kitty.   그녀의 친구들은 그녀를 Kitty라고 부른다.

→ ____

LEVEL UP

 우리말과 같은 뜻이 되도록 빈칸에 알맞은 말을 쓰세요.

1 Mom _____made_____ my sister _____a_____ _____sweater_____.
엄마는 내 여동생에게 스웨터를 만들어주셨다.

2 Jim _____________ _____________ _____________ a gift.
Jim은 그의 친구에게 선물을 보냈다.

3 The rain _____________ _____________ _____________.
비가 우리를 젖게 했다.

4 She found _____________ _____________ _____________.
그녀는 그 일이 따분하다고 느꼈다.

5 I _____________ him _____________ _____________.
나는 그에게 이메일을 보냈다.

6 Homework often _____________ _____________ _____________.
숙제는 종종 나를 지치게 한다.

B 우리말과 같은 뜻이 되도록 빈칸에 알맞은 말을 쓰세요.

1 Harry _____ sent _____ _____ her _____ _____ some _____ _____ flowers _____ .
Harry는 그녀에게 꽃을 좀 보냈다.

2 You _____________ _____________ _____________ .
너는 나를 행복하게 만든다.

3 I'll _____________ _____________ _____________ _____________ photos.
내가 가장 좋아하는 사진들을 너에게 보여줄게.

4 He _____________ _____________ _____________ _____________ .
그는 그 상자를 자주색으로 칠했다.

5 My friend _____________ me _____________ _____________ .
내 친구가 내게 선물을 주었다.

6 My brother told _____________ _____________ _____________ .
우리 형은 나에게 자신의 계획을 말했다.

7 Please _____________ _____________ _____________ _____________ .
그에게 티켓들을 보내세요.

8 The cookies _____________ _____________ _____________ .
그 과자는 그녀를 목마르게 했다.

9 They _____________ _____________ _____________ John.
그들은 그들의 아들 이름을 John이라고 지었다.

10 They _____________ _____________ _____________ _____________ .
그들은 Alex에게 그 일자리를 제안했다.

[1~3] (   ) 안에서 알맞은 것을 고르세요.

1 The cake tastes (① sweet / ② sweetly).

2 Dogs bark (① loud / ② loudly) in the yard.

3 The girl looks (① beautiful / ② beautifully).

4 어법상 올바른 문장을 고르세요.

① He seems nicely.

② You look tire.

③ The steak smells good.

④ He feels happily.

5 밑줄 친 부분을 바르게 고친 것을 고르세요.

I miss they so much.

① their   ② they're   ③ them   ④ themselves

6 밑줄 친 부분이 <u>어색한</u> 것을 고르세요.

① We baked <u>some cookies</u>.

② He posted <u>a message</u> on a website.

③ She was eating <u>a sandwich</u>.

④ I didn't <u>any food eat</u>.

7 다음 문장에서 him이 들어갈 위치를 고르세요.

I am going ① to ② meet ③ in the library ④ at 10:00.

[8~9] 빈칸에 들어갈 수 <u>없는</u> 말을 고르세요.

8 It sounds ____________.

① good　　② exciting　　③ fun　　④ greatly

9 Everyone feels ____________ at times.

① sad　　② happy　　③ lonely　　④ badly

10 빈칸에 공통으로 알맞은 말을 고르세요.

> · My friend gave ______________ a present.
> · My brother told ______________ his plans.

① me ② to me ③ I ④ mine

11 빈칸에 들어갈 말이 바르게 짝지어진 것을 고르세요.

> · Tony finds her new song ______________.
> · The song made him ______________.

① amazingly – happy ② amazing – happy

③ amazing – happily ④ amazingly – happily

12 밑줄 친 부분이 올바른 것을 고르세요.

① My sister taught to me English.

② David sent for his friend a gift.

③ My mom bought to me a bike.

④ I will tell you the story.

13 우리말을 영어로 바르게 옮긴 것을 고르세요.

> 그 소식은 그녀를 슬프게 했다.

① The news made she sad.

② The news made her sadly.

③ The news made her sad.

④ The news made sad her.

14 어법상 <u>틀린</u> 부분을 찾아 바르게 고쳐 쓰세요.

Public speaking makes David nervously.

_________________________ ➔ _________________________

15 우리말과 같은 뜻이 되도록 빈칸에 알맞은 말을 쓰세요.

나는 그에게 그 사진들을 보여주지 않았다.

➔ I _____________ _____________ _____________ the photos.

16 그림을 보고 밑줄 친 부분을 바르게 고쳐 쓰세요. (for는 사용하지 마세요.)

Today is Susan's birthday.

Tony bought (1) <u>some flowers she</u>.

He (2) <u>gave she</u> a gift, too.

It made her (3) <u>happiness</u>.

She (4) <u>gave to him</u> a big smile.

He also smiled at her.

(1) _________________________________

(2) _________________________________

(3) _________________________________

(4) _________________________________

1 밑줄 친 about의 의미가 나머지와 다른 것을 고르세요.

① He studied about the desert.

② She worked for about an hour.

③ She wrote a book about flowers.

④ He teaches students about stars.

2 다음 문장에서 in이 들어갈 위치를 고르세요.

I am going to ① meet ② her ③ the park ④ at 3 p.m.

[3~4] 우리말과 같은 뜻이 되도록 빈칸에 들어갈 알맞은 말을 고르세요.

3

There is a bakery _______ the flower shop.
(꽃집 옆에 제과점이 있다.)

① under ② next to

③ between ④ in front of

4

I will learn how to swim _______ the vacation.
(나는 방학 동안 수영을 배울 것이다.)

① by ② for

③ until ④ during

[5~6] 빈칸에 공통으로 알맞은 말을 고르세요.

5

- A cat is sitting _______ the roof.
- Jenny invited her friends _______ her birthday.

① in ② at

③ on ④ under

6

- My mother gave _______ a present.
- My sister showed _______ her dress.

① I ② me

③ to me ④ mine

7 어법상 <u>틀린</u> 문장을 고르세요.

① There is a cat on the sofa.

② She is climbing up the ladder.

③ An orange fell to the ground.

④ There is a child between they.

8 어법상 올바른 문장을 고르세요.

① He looks tire.

② She seems nicely.

③ The boy felt happily.

④ The pasta tastes good.

[9~10] 빈칸에 들어갈 말이 바르게 짝지어진 것을 고르세요.

9
- There is a hospital _______ the park.
- She has to finish the work _______ noon.

① between – next to

② in front of – by

③ behind – during

④ under – until

10
- Make your point _______.
- The news made her _______.

① clear – happy

② cleared – happy

③ clear – happily

④ clearly – happily

11 빈칸에 on을 쓸 수 <u>없는</u> 문장을 고르세요.

① It rained _______ a week.

② She goes to church _______ Sunday.

③ He got some gifts _______ his birthday.

④ They went to the zoo _______ May 7th.

12 밑줄 친 부분이 올바른 것을 고르세요.

① He <u>gave me</u> some money.

② I <u>taught to my brother</u> math.

③ Paul <u>sent for her</u> some flowers.

④ My uncle <u>bought to me</u> a computer.

[13~14] 우리말을 영어로 바르게 옮긴 것을 고르세요.

13 우리는 물 없이 살 수 없다.

① We cannot live like water.

② We cannot live with water.

③ We cannot live about water.

④ We cannot live without water.

14 그 소식은 우리들을 슬프게 했다.

① The news made us sad.

② The news made sad us.

③ The news made we sad.

④ The news made us sadly.

15 주어진 문장의 밑줄 친 in과 쓰임이 다른 것을 고르세요.

Many children are playing <u>in</u> the park.

① Mr. Bean lives <u>in</u> London.

② He exercises <u>in</u> the morning.

③ There is a piano <u>in</u> the living room.

④ There are lots of countries <u>in</u> Asia.

16 밑줄 친 부분을 바르게 고친 것을 고르세요.

The old man missed <u>they</u> so much.

① their ② them

③ they're ④ themselves

[17~18] 빈칸에 들어갈 수 <u>없는</u> 말을 고르세요.

17 Alice felt _______ today.

① bored ② sad

③ lonely ④ greatly

18 The dress looks _______.

① nice ② strange

③ small ④ beautifully

그는 방학 동안 스케이트를 배울 것이다.
(how to skate / will / the vacation / during / learn / he / .)

____

I went for Busan to Hong Kong by ship. (나는 배로 부산에서 홍콩으로 갔다.)

_______________ ➙ _______________

할머니는 나에게 장갑을 만들어 주셨다.

➙ My grandmother ___________
___________ gloves.

보기	bought	sang	show
	happy	tasty	next to

I'll ___________ you my birthday picture. Charlie is my best friend and he is ___________ me. He ___________ me a cap. Jane is between Charlie and my mom. She ___________ me a beautiful song. The food was fresh and ___________. All of them made me ___________.

MEMO

MEMO

지은이

NE능률 영어교육연구소

NE능률 영어교육연구소는 혁신적이며 효율적인 영어 교재를 개발하고
영어 학습의 질을 한 단계 높이고자 노력하는 NE능률의 연구 조직입니다.

초등 Grammar Inside 〈6권〉

펴 낸 이	주민홍
펴 낸 곳	서울특별시 마포구 월드컵북로 396(상암동) 누리꿈스퀘어 비즈니스타워 10층
	㈜)NE능률 (우편번호 03925)
펴 낸 날	2022년 1월 5일 초판 제1쇄 발행
전　　화	02 2014 7114
팩　　스	02 3142 0356
홈 페 이 지	www.neungyule.com
등록번호	제1-68호
I S B N	979-11-253-3715-7 63740
정　　가	13,000원

NE 능률

고객센터

교재 내용 문의 : contact.nebooks.co.kr (별도의 가입 절차 없이 작성 가능)
제품 구매, 교환, 불량, 반품 문의 : 02-2014-7114
☎ 전화문의는 본사 업무시간 중에만 가능합니다.

[01~03] 빈칸에 들어갈 알맞은 말을 고르세요.

01

I hope _________ Canada someday.

① visit ② visited
③ to visit ④ visiting
⑤ will visit

02

It is wrong _________ a lie.

① to tell ② tell
③ told ④ telling
⑤ will tell

03

Would you mind _________ seats?

① exchange ② exchanged
③ exchanging ④ to exchange
⑤ will exchange

[04~05] 빈칸에 들어갈 수 없는 말을 고르세요.

04

I want _________.

① a new phone ② to sleep
③ to be a singer ④ something to eat
⑤ buy a computer

05

She began _________.

① playing the piano ② climb mountains
③ to dance ④ to play the guitar
⑤ singing

[06~07] 밑줄 친 부분의 쓰임이 나머지와 다른 것을 고르세요.

06

① He saves money to travel.
② I went there to see Jane.
③ She ran to catch the bus.
④ I need some water to drink.
⑤ I went out to watch a movie.

07

① My dad gave up smoking.
② I enjoy travelling.
③ She finished doing the dishes.
④ He avoids making a decision.
⑤ She is studying English.

08 빈칸에 by가 들어갈 수 없는 것을 고르세요.

① She goes to school _________ bus.
② I will finish the work _________ noon.
③ We will wait _________ Saturday.
④ He went to Paris _________ airplane.
⑤ I will call you _________ Thursday.

[09~10] 빈칸에 들어갈 말이 바르게 짝지어진 것을 고르세요.

09

• I got up _________ 7 o'clock.
• She goes to church _________ Sunday.

① at – at ② at – on
③ at – in ④ in – on
⑤ in – for

10

• Let's meet _________ the bus stop.
• My uncle lives _________ New York.

① at – in ② at – on
③ in – at ④ in – on
⑤ on – in

[11~13] 밑줄 친 부분이 어색한 것을 고르세요.

11
① My sister was born in 2015.
② Don't talk during the exam.
③ He sat down in front of she.
④ It rained for two hours.
⑤ Can I stay until the weekend?

12
① The puppy looks cute.
② The cake tastes sweet.
③ He feels bored.
④ The bus came too lately.
⑤ His new neighbors seem nice.

13
① Her song made him happy.
② They elected the chairperson him.
③ I find Tom really smart.
④ She always keeps her room clean.
⑤ Don't call me a liar.

14 우리말을 영어로 바르게 옮긴 것을 고르세요.

그는 그 일이 흥미롭다고 여겼다.

① He found the work interest.
② He found the work interested.
③ He found the work interesting.
④ He found the work interestingly.
⑤ He found interesting the work.

15 어법상 틀린 문장을 고르세요.
① I sent him an email.
② John told me a secret.
③ He bought me a cap.
④ Mary showed me her pictures.
⑤ Mom made to my sister a sweater.

16 우리말과 같은 뜻이 되도록 빈칸에 알맞은 말을 쓰세요.

그는 약 7시간 동안 잤다.

→ He slept for ______________ seven hours.

17 어법상 틀린 부분을 찾아 바르게 고쳐 쓰세요.

The young singer became famously.

________________ → ________________

[18~19] 우리말과 같은 뜻이 되도록 주어진 말을 바르게 배열하세요.

18
어젯밤에는 바람이 불었다.
(last night / windy / was / it / .)

→ ________________________________

19
나는 내 방을 파란색으로 칠하고 싶다.
(I / want / paint / to / blue / my room / .)

→ ________________________________

20 주어진 말을 이용하여 빈칸에 알맞은 말을 쓰세요.

Stop ______________ with your food! (play)

총괄평가 02회

이름:

점수:

[01~03] 빈칸에 들어갈 알맞은 말을 고르세요.

01

The boy talked __________.

① loud   ② loudly
③ loudness   ④ to be loud
⑤ to be loudly

02

The weather __________ today.

① looks coldly   ② looks cold
③ looks coldness   ④ looking cold
⑤ looking coldly

03

I found the movie __________.

① excitingly   ② exciting
③ to be excitedly   ④ excitement
⑤ excite

[04~05] 빈칸에 들어갈 수 <u>없는</u> 말을 고르세요.

04

I like __________.

① climbing mountains   ② playing soccer
③ to watch movies   ④ baseball
⑤ eat hamburgers

05

The girl started __________.

① to cry   ② walking
③ to laughing   ④ singing
⑤ to dance

[06~07] 밑줄 친 부분의 쓰임이 나머지와 <u>다른</u> 것을 고르세요.

06
① <u>It</u> is fun to sing.
② <u>It</u> is wrong to tell a lie.
③ <u>It</u> is windy today.
④ <u>It</u> is exciting to see fireworks.
⑤ <u>It</u> is easy to bake a cake.

07
① I have no money <u>to spend</u>.
② I want something <u>to eat</u>.
③ I don't have anything <u>to wear</u>.
④ She gave me a book <u>to read</u>.
⑤ I went to the library <u>to study</u>.

08 빈칸에 in이 들어갈 수 <u>없는</u> 것을 고르세요.
① He was born __________ 2010.
② My cousin lives __________ Canada.
③ The book is __________ the backpack.
④ She goes to the park __________ Sunday.
⑤ Which is the largest city __________ the world?

[09~10] 빈칸에 들어갈 말이 바르게 짝지어진 것을 고르세요.

09

• He is climbing __________ the ladder.
• The calendar is falling __________.

① up – down   ② from – down
③ down – up   ④ from – to
⑤ up – to

10

• Look at the girl __________ blond hair.
• The baby smiles __________ an angel.

① like – with   ② with – like
③ in – with   ④ to – like
⑤ on – like

[11~13] 밑줄 친 부분이 어색한 것을 고르세요.

11
① I walked here from home.
② I usually walk to school.
③ He is swimming across the river.
④ The store is open from 9 a.m. by 10 p.m.
⑤ The train is going through the tunnel.

12
① Dancing is fun.
② Making cookies is not difficult.
③ I hate cycling.
④ What she really loves is skiing.
⑤ He stopped to looking at the painting.

13
① Her dream is to be a writer.
② His job is to sell computers.
③ She ran to avoid to be late.
④ I went there to see Cathy.
⑤ Jane learned to ride a bike.

14 우리말을 영어로 바르게 옮긴 것을 고르세요.

그것을 다시 한번 설명해 주시겠어요?

① Would you mind explain that again?
② Would you mind to explain that again?
③ Would you mind explaining that again?
④ Would you mind to explaining that again?
⑤ Would you mind will explain that again?

15 어법상 틀린 문장을 고르세요.

① The food was tasty and fresh.
② The medicine tastes bitter.
③ Do you feel better now?
④ The sky turned darkly after lunch.
⑤ They practice soccer on Saturday.

16 우리말과 같은 뜻이 되도록 빈칸에 알맞은 말을 쓰세요.

내일까지 기다리자.

→ Let's wait ______________ tomorrow.

17 어법상 틀린 부분을 찾아 바르게 고쳐 쓰세요.

The news made them sadly.

________________ → ________________

[18~19] 우리말과 같은 뜻이 되도록 주어진 말을 바르게 배열하세요.

18
시간이 지나서 그들이 틀렸다는 것이 밝혀졌다.
(time / them / wrong / proved / .)

→ ________________________________

19
구멍을 통해 햇빛이 들어온다.
(the hole / through / sunlight / comes in / .)

→ ________________________________

20 주어진 말을 이용하여 빈칸에 알맞은 말을 쓰세요.

It is wrong ______________ animals. (hurt)

초등 Grammar Inside

Answer Key

6

NE

초등

Grammar Inside

Student Book
Answer Key

6

Unit 01   명사처럼 쓰이는 to부정사

CHECK UP   p.9

A
1. to sleep
2. to think
3. to act
4. to see
5. to play
6. to eat
7. to come
8. to be
9. to swim
10. to go

B
1. to sleep, ⓑ
2. To think, To act, ⓐ
3. to act, ⓐ
4. to be, ⓒ
5. to play, ⓑ
6. to sell, ⓒ

Unit 02   형용사와 부사처럼 쓰이는 to부정사

CHECK UP   p.11

A   1. ⓑ   2. ⓐ   3. ⓐ   4. ⓑ   5. ⓐ

해석
1. 그녀는 버스를 잡기 위해 달렸다.
2. 나는 입을 것이 아무것도 없다.
3. 나는 전화할 친구가 있다.
4. 그는 일을 찾기 위해 호주로 갈 것이다.
5. 너는 문을 열 번호를 알고 있니?

B   1. to read   2. to drink   3. to watch   4. to buy

LET'S PRACTICE 1   p.12

A
1. to ride
2. to swim
3. to visit
4. to become
5. to travel
6. to leave

B
1. to tell
2. to see
3. to join
4. to cry
5. to visit
6. to collect

LET'S PRACTICE 2   p.13

A
1. to study
2. to spend
3. to drink
4. to do
5. to sell
6. to play

B
1. to arrive
2. to give
3. to start
4. to drink
5. to buy
6. to study

STEP UP 1   p.14

A
1. to take
2. to turn off
3. to visit
4. to meet
5. to play
6. to bake
7. to draw
8. to see
9. to get
10. to eat
11. to help
12. to look for

B
1. to travel
2. to lose
3. to speak
4. to get
5. to drink
6. to buy
7. to buy
8. to wear
9. to look
10. to write
11. to do
12. to read

STEP UP 2   p.16

A
1. like to play
2. want to go
3. is to travel
4. is to lose
5. fun to swim
6. wrong to hurt
7. time to close
8. money to buy
9. something to read
10. hard to speak
11. there to fix
12. home to get

B
1. to go
2. to visit
3. to draw
4. to give
5. to play
6. to pass

STEP UP 3   p.18

A
1. something to tell
2. a promise to visit
3. some money to spend
4. to download the apps
5. to have lunch
6. to travel the world
7. learned to drive
8. to see the games
9. to be a singer
10. to teach English

B
1. to drive
2. to become
3. to visit
4. to arrive
5. to do
6. to get
7. to buy
8. to say

STEP UP 4   p.20

A
1. It is wrong to hurt animals.
2. It is time to go home.
3. He forgot to turn off the switch.
4. We didn't expect to see each other.
5. My favorite thing is to listen to music.
6. It is easy to solve the problem.
7. I bought a pencil to draw a picture.

8. His wish is to visit the Blue House.

9. I need something to eat.

10. He practices hard to become better.

B
1. He ran to catch the train.

2. Her dream is to be a writer.

3. His job is to sell books.

4. I found a good place to study.

5. He likes to play tennis.

6. We have no time to waste.

7. He is saving money to go to London.

8. I went there to play soccer.

9. I have a friend to help me.

10. I need time to check my email.

LEVEL UP
p.22

A
1. like to travel
2. went, to drink
3. to buy
4. time to close
5. decided to join
6. to draw a picture

B
1. time to travel
2. It is, to swim
3. to turn off
4. time to start
5. to play basketball
6. anything to wear
7. to open the door
8. learned to ride
9. to arrive
10. to leave early
11. started[began] to cry
12. stopped to look

Chapter 01 REVIEW TEST
p.24

1. ① **2.** ① **3.** ② **4.** ③ **5.** ① **6.** ② **7.** ②
8. ④ **9.** ④ **10.** ① **11.** ② **12.** ④ **13.** ②
14. downloading → download **15.** (1) to go (2)
to eat **16.** to play, to be, to become, to learn, to
catch, to hit

1 주어 자리에 It이 있으므로 뒤에는 to부정사가 형태가 자
연스럽다.

2 be동사 뒤에 보어로는 to부정사가 올 수 있으므로 to sell
이 알맞다.

3 money를 뒤에서 꾸며주는 말로는 to부정사 올 수 있으므
로 to spend가 알맞다.

4 ① studying → to study ② eat → to eat ④ catching
→ catch

5 '그녀는 불을 끄는 것을 잊어버렸다'는 의미가 자연스러우
므로 「forgot + to부정사」 형태가 알맞다.

6 ② emails를 뒤에서 꾸며주는 to부정사가 적절하므로 to
writing은 to write가 되어야 한다.

7 ②는 '~할'이라는 뜻으로 형용사 역할을 하고 있고, ①, ③,
④는 '~하는 것'이라는 뜻으로 명사(목적어) 역할을 하고

있다.

8 decided의 목적어로 「to + 동사원형」이 적절하므로, ④
bought it은 buy it으로 고쳐야 한다.

9 want의 목적어로는 to부정사나 명사가 올 수 있으므로 ④
see는 to see로 고쳐야 한다.

10 첫 문장은 '뉴스를 얻는 가장 좋은 방법'이란 뜻으로 the
best way를 꾸며주는 to get이 알맞다. 두 번째 문장은
'좋은 성적을 얻기 위해'라는 뜻으로 목적을 나타내는 to부
정사인 to get이 알맞다.

11 첫 문장은 주어 자리에 It이 있으므로 뒤에는 to부정사인
to hurt가 오는 것이 알맞다. 두 번째 문장은 '~하기 위해'
라는 뜻의 to부정사가 오는 것이 알맞다.

12 ① to losing → to lose ② to reading → to read ③
fixed → to fix

13 some emails를 꾸며주는 「to + 동사원형」 형태가 뒤에 오
는 것이 알맞다.

14 목적을 나타내는 to부정사가 와야 하므로, downloading
은 download로 고쳐야 한다.

15 (1) want 뒤에는 to부정사가 오므로 to go가 알맞다. (2)
something을 꾸며주는 to eat이 알맞다.

16 주어진 동사 앞에 to를 넣어 「to + 동사원형」 형태로 쓴다.

Chapter 02 동명사

Unit 01　동명사의 형태와 역할

CHECK UP
p.31

A
1. coming
2. riding
3. swimming
4. believing
5. dancing
6. eating
7. taking
8. listening
9. beginning
10. winning

B
1. running, ⓑ
2. Swimming, ⓐ
3. Exercising, ⓐ
4. skiing, ⓒ
5. doing, ⓑ
6. jumping, ⓒ

Unit 02　목적어로 쓰이는 동명사와 to부정사

CHECK UP
p.33

A
1. ○　2. X　3. ○　4. ○　5. ○　6. X
7. X　8. ○　9. X　10. ○

B
1. playing
2. to dance
3. waiting
4. winning

LET'S PRACTICE 1　　　　p.34

A　1. ⓑ　2. ⓑ　3. ⓐ　4. ⓐ　5. ⓑ　6. ⓑ

B　1. Writing　2. cooking　3. painting
　　4. Reading　5. walking

LET'S PRACTICE 2　　　　p.35

A　1. running　2. crying　3. meeting
　　4. to stay　5. to visit

B　1. ○　2. X　3. ○　4. ○　5. X　6. X

STEP UP 1　　　　p.36

A　1. skiing　　2. Cycling　　3. living
　　4. buying　　5. swimming　6. playing
　　7. Listening　8. taking　　9. waiting
　　10. Teaching　11. making　　12. opening

B　1. turning　　2. to feel　　3. meeting
　　4. trying　　5. reading　　6. shouting
　　7. to eat　　8. to stay　　9. to lose
　　10. to leave　11. going

STEP UP 2　　　　p.38

A　1. cycling[to cycle]　　　2. doing
　　3. working　4. writing　5. talking
　　6. to go　7. explaining　8. to visit
　　9. leaving[to leave]　　10. to drink
　　11. to arrive　12. to call

B　1. Swimming　2. Skiing　3. watching
　　4. Making　5. playing　6. Walking

STEP UP 3　　　　p.40

A　1. Traveling by airplane
　　2. enjoys watching sports
　　3. listening to music
　　4. Swimming is good for
　　5. hates making mistakes
　　6. enjoy working with
　　7. Writing in English
　　8. doesn't like studying
　　9. loves playing soccer
　　10. gave up teaching

B　1. Do you mind turning down the music?
　　2. She needs to feel loved.
　　3. I enjoy visiting new places.
　　4. He keeps trying to talk to me.
　　5. Did you finish reading this book?
　　6. Stop talking and listen!
　　7. What do you want to do tomorrow?
　　8. I'm planning to stay here.
　　9. He needs to lose a pound or two.
　　10. I was hoping to leave work early today.

STEP UP 4　　　　p.42

A　1. His hobby is playing basketball.
　　2. She enjoys walking daily.
　　3. I go swimming once a week.
　　4. I hate doing my homework.
　　5. Would you mind opening the door?
　　6. They started to run.
　　7. I hate to wait for the train.
　　8. Cleaning my room is boring.
　　9. I finished doing the dishes.
　　10. He likes climbing mountains.

B　1. I keep making the same mistake.
　　2. Would you mind exchanging seats?
　　3. I want to be alone.
　　4. They hope to succeed.
　　5. Mr. Jones wishes to see you.
　　6. I plan to go fishing.
　　7. We chose to go by bus.
　　8. She decided to grow her hair.
　　9. He promised to come back.
　　10. I like climbing[to climb] mountains.

LEVEL UP　　　　p.44

A　1. Riding a bike　2. Writing in English
　　3. enjoy walking　4. finish reading
　　5. keep running　6. hate, the dishes

B　1. enjoy skiing　2. Stop playing
　　3. making friends　4. Teaching, learning
　　5. go swimming
　　6. avoid going shopping
　　7. needs to lose　8. planning to stay
　　9. trying to win
　　10. enjoy meeting people
　　11. need to feel
　　12. mind turning down

1. ②　**2.** ②　**3.** ②　**4.** ③　**5.** ①　**6.** ②　**7.** ②　**8.** ④
9. ④　**10.** ①　**11.** ③　**12.** ④　**13.** ②
14. to smoke → smoking　**15.** (1) turning　(2) to turn　**16.** to watch, going, to see, going

1　보어로는 동명사나 to부정사가 올 수 있으므로 watching이나 to watch가 와야 한다.

2　동명사는 주어가 될 수 있고 자체의 목적어를 취할 수 있으므로 Making이 알맞다.

3　동사 keep은 동명사를 목적어로 취하므로 working이 알맞다.

4　① to wash → washing ② to talk → talking ④ going → go

5　그는 '쓰기를 멈추고 잠들었다'는 의미가 자연스러우므로 「stop + 동명사」 형태가 알맞다.

6　② hope는 to부정사를 목적어로 취하는 동사이므로 arriving은 to arrive가 되어야 한다.

7　②의 playing은 be동사와 함께 현재진행형임을 나타내고, 나머지는 동명사로 쓰였다.

8　동사 want, plan, promise 뒤에는 to부정사를 쓰고, mind 뒤에는 동명사를 쓴다.

9　④ 동명사가 문장의 주어로 쓰일 때는 단수 취급한다.

10　begin 뒤에는 목적어로 동명사나 to부정사를 쓸 수 있다. avoid, give up, finish 뒤에는 목적어로 동명사를 쓰고 to부정사는 쓸 수 없다.

11　동사 keep 뒤에는 동명사를, promise 뒤에는 to부정사를 목적어로 쓴다.

12　① to studying → studying 혹은 to study ② to work → working ③ to teach → teaching

13　이야기하는 것을 그만 두라고 했으므로, stop 뒤에는 to부정사가 아니라 동명사인 talking이 와야 한다. 동사는 Stop ~ and listen 형태의 명령문으로 나열되는 것이 적절하다.

14　give up은 목적어로 동명사를 취한다.

15　(1) mind 뒤에는 동명사가 오므로 turning이 적절하다. (2) want 다음에는 to부정사가 오므로 to turn이 적절하다.

16　빈칸에 맞게 like, want 다음에는 to부정사를 목적어로 쓰고, enjoy, hate 다음에는 동명사를 목적어로 쓴다.

1. ④　**2.** ②　**3.** ②　**4.** ①　**5.** ③　**6.** ①　**7.** ②　**8.** ③
9. ②　**10.** ④　**11.** ①　**12.** ③　**13.** ④　**14.** ①　**15.** ①
16. ②　**17.** ③　**18.** ②　**19.** It is dangerous to swim in the river.　**20.** to wait → waiting　**21.** to become a great pianist　**22.** riding, to ride, to read, to become, to go, getting up, to read

1　①, ②, ③은 목적어로 쓰인 명사적 용법이고, ④는 time을 꾸며주는 형용사적 용법이다.

2　①, ③, ④는 동명사(~하는 것)로 쓰였으나, ②는 현재진행형(~하는 중이다)으로 쓰였다.

3　[보기]와 ②는 목적을 나타내는 부사적 용법으로 쓰였다. ①은 주어(명사적 용법), ③과 ④는 형용사적 용법의 to부정사이다.

4　동사는 문장의 주어로 쓰일 수 없으므로 to부정사나 동명사의 형태로 바꿔야 한다.

5　finish는 동명사를 목적어로 쓰는 동사이다.

6　hate나 like 다음에는 목적어로 동명사(cleaning)나 to부정사(to clean)를 쓴다.

7　like의 목적어로 쓰인 동명사는 to부정사로 바꿔 쓸 수 있다.

8　enjoy는 동명사를 목적어로 쓰는 동사이고, want, hope, decide는 to부정사를 목적어로 쓰는 동사이다.

9　'~하는 것을 멈추다'라는 뜻이 자연스러우므로 빈칸에는 동명사 working이 알맞다.

10　① to being → to be　② becoming → to become　③ buy → to buy

11　decided의 목적어로는 to부정사가 쓰이므로 for는 to로 바꿔야 한다.

12　③ 주어로 쓰인 동명사는 단수 취급한다. are → is

13　④ to playing → to play

14　need는 목적어로 to부정사를 쓴다.

15　첫 번째 문장은 '마지막 버스를 타기 위해' 달린 것이므로 목적을 나타내는 to부정사인 to catch가 알맞다. 두 번째 문장은 avoid가 동명사를 목적어로 취하므로 meeting이 알맞다.

16　첫 문장은 주어 자리에 It이 있으므로 뒤에는 to부정사인 to swim이 오는 것이 알맞다. 두 번째 문장은 '~하기 위해'라는 뜻의 to부정사가 오는 것이 알맞다.

17　첫 문장의 동사 keep은 목적어로 동명사를 쓴다. 두 번째 문장의 동사 promise는 to부정사를 목적어로 쓴다.

18　첫 문장은 '불을 피우기'란 뜻으로 동사 decided의 목적어로 쓰인 to make가 알맞다. 두 번째 문장은 '돈을 벌기 위해'라는 뜻으로 목적을 나타내는 부정사 to make가 알맞다.

19　주어 자리에 it을 쓰고 to부정사는 뒤에 놓아 It is dangerous to swim ~ 순으로 배열한다.

20　mind(꺼리다, 싫어하다)는 동명사만을 목적어로 쓰는 동사이므로 뒤의 to wait를 waiting으로 고쳐야 한다.

21　앞 문장의 동사 practices를 부사처럼 꾸며 주는 to부정사를 사용하여 뒷 문장을 연결한다. 이때의 to부정사는 '~하기 위해, ~하려고'라는 뜻으로 목적을 나타낸다.

22　enjoy, hates 다음에는 주어진 동사의 동명사형을 쓰고, 나머지 문장에는 주어진 동사의 to부정사 형태를 써서 빈칸에 맞게 문장을 완성한다.

Chapter 03 전치사

Unit 01 시간의 전치사

CHECK UP p.57

A 1. ⓐ 2. ⓐ 3. ⓑ 4. ⓑ 5. ⓐ 6. ⓑ

B 1. during 2. for 3. by 4. until

Unit 02 장소의 전치사

CHECK UP p.59

A 1. in 2. at 3. at 4. at 5. in 6. in

B 1. behind 2. in 3. between
4. in front of 5. under 6. next to

해석
1 그는 그의 딸 뒤에 있다.
2 사과 몇 개가 바구니 안에 있다.
3 그 아이는 그녀의 부모님 사이에 있다.
4 그는 불 앞에 있다.
5 개 한 마리가 침대 아래에서 자고 있다.
6 그들은 트리 옆에 있다.

LET'S PRACTICE 1 p.60

A 1. in 2. on 3. on 4. at 5. in 6. at

B 1. in 2. during 3. by 4. for 5. on
6. until

LET'S PRACTICE 2 p.61

A 1. in 2. under 3. in front of 4. at 5. on

B 1. between 2. under 3. behind 4. next to

STEP UP 1 p.62

A 1. in 2. until 3. on 4. in 5. At 6. by
7. until 8. on 9. for 10. in 11. at
12. for

B 1. in 2. on 3. next to

4. on 5. between 6. at
7. under 8. behind 9. in front of
10. in 11. under 12. next to

STEP UP 2 p.64

A 1. for 2. by 3. in 4. on 5. until
6. during 7. in front of 8. between
9. next to 10. behind

B 1. at 2. in 3. at 4. on 5. at 6. on

STEP UP 3 p.66

A
1. met Fred at seven
2. between the two mountains
3. the living room on Saturday
4. in the sea
5. during the summer
6. on the wall
7. many stars at night
8. behind the sofa
9. until the weekend
10. in front of the hospital

B
1. on the table
2. during the day
3. behind the box
4. at 10 o'clock
5. under the tree
6. for three years
7. in front of the bookstore
8. during the break
9. next to the computer
10. between the two buildings

STEP UP 4 p.68

A
1. The museum closes at 5 p.m.
2. A bird is sitting on your hat.
3. It rained a lot during the morning.
4. The river flows under the bridge.
5. I will go camping on Saturday.
6. There is a tower in front of the temple.
7. Keep studying until 3 p.m.
8. There is a lake between the two cities.
9. My younger brother was born in 2017.
10. There is a market next to the gym.

B 1. There is a black cat on the roof.
2. I get up at 7 every morning.
3. There are some potatoes in the box.
4. You can stay here until the weekend.
5. There is a parking lot behind the building.
6. My father worked in Busan for a year.
7. I want to get many gifts on Christmas.
8. She is smiling between her parents.
9. The hunter lived in the forest.
10. He was born in August.

LEVEL UP p.70

A 1. at 2. for 3. in front of 4. until 5. on
6. between

B 1. next to the library 2. by Thursday
3. in the evening 4. behind the house
5. many pyramids in 6. in the summer
7. under the bed 8. in the spring
9. on the ground 10. at the airport

Unit 03 방향의 전치사

CHECK UP p.73

A 1. up 2. across 3. down 4. to
5. through 6. from

B 1. ⓑ 2. ⓐ 3. ⓓ 4. ⓒ

Unit 04 기타 전치사

CHECK UP p.75

A 1. ⓒ 2. ⓓ 3. ⓔ 4. ⓐ 5. ⓑ

B 1. without 2. by 3. like 4. about

LET'S PRACTICE 1 p.76

A 1. ⓐ 2. ⓑ 3. ⓑ 4. ⓐ 5. ⓑ

B 1. across 2. up 3. through 4. from, to
5. down

LET'S PRACTICE 2 p.77

A 1. without 2. like 3. by 4. on
5. with

B 1. about 2. without 3. by 4. like

STEP UP 1 p.78

A 1. down 2. about 3. through 4. without
5. from 6. by 7. up 8. with
9. across 10. like 11. to 12. down

B 1. through 2. up 3. about 4. by
5. without 6. with 7. across 8. to
9. from 10. with 11. down 12. through

STEP UP 2 p.80

A 1. like 2. by 3. with 4. about
5. without 6. to 7. up 8. through
9. down 10. from

B 1. up 2. like 3. by 4. down
5. across 6. about

STEP UP 3 p.82

A 1. flying up in the sky
2. study math with my friend
3. school from my house
4. a girl with red hair
5. smiles like an angel
6. going through the tunnel
7. like traveling by bus
8. running down the hill
9. a poem about flowers
10. go shopping without me

B 1. the island by ship
2. swimming across the lake
3. going through the tunnel
4. walked to the museum
5. coming down the stairs
6. played soccer with his friends
7. cooked pasta without her help
8. came in through the window
9. flying high
10. looks like a pumpkin

A
1. She had dinner with her family.
2. He goes to school by bicycle.
3. She drove through the village.
4. She ran across the road.
5. She is reading a book about Korean history.
6. My brother goes to school on foot.
7. He is climbing up the ladder.
8. The ducks are swimming across the pond.
9. She went out without a mask.
10. The cat fell from the roof.

B
1. The leaf is falling down.
2. She ran across the playground.
3. Don't go camping without me.
4. This candy tastes like an orange.
5. A mosquito came in through the hole.
6. I want to go shopping with him.
7. They are talking about cars.
8. An apple fell from the tree.
9. Butterflies fly from flower to flower.
10. A motorcycle is going up the hill.

LEVEL UP　　　　　　　　　　p.86

A
1. across the street　2. through the hole
3. like a star　4. with blond hair
5. up the wall　6. by subway

B
1. go to the zoo
2. ran across the square
3. live without love
4. down to the ground
5. by airplane[plane]
6. with big eyes
7. about your dream
8. like an angel
9. climbing up the ladder
10. through the tunnel

Chapter 03 REVIEW TEST　　　p.88

1. ①　**2.** ②　**3.** ①　**4.** ④　**5.** ③　**6.** ①　**7.** ③　**8.** ④
9. ③　**10.** ④　**11.** ②　**12.** ④　**13.** ④
14. across → through　**15.** The train runs from Seoul to Chuncheon.　**16.** between, under, on, behind

1　'~ 옆에'라는 의미의 전치사는 next to이다.
2　어떤 일이 얼마 동안(how long) 계속되었는지를 말할 때는 전치사 for를 쓴다.
3　'가로질러'라는 의미의 전치사는 across이다.
4　until은 언제까지 '계속'되는 것을 말할 때 쓰이고, by는 '~보다 늦지 않게'라는 뜻으로 말할 때 쓰인다.
5　between은 '~ 사이에'의 의미이다.
6　첫 번째 빈칸에는 도착지 앞에 쓰여 '~로, ~에'의 의미를 나타내는 to가, 두 번째 빈칸에는 교통수단 앞에 쓰여 '~를 타고'의 의미를 나타내는 by가, 세 번째 빈칸에는 요일 앞에 쓰여 '~에'의 의미를 나타내는 on이 알맞다.
7　전치사 on은 장소를 나타낼 때는 '~ 위에'라는 뜻으로, 요일을 나타낼 때는 '~에'라는 뜻으로 쓰인다.
8　첫 번째 빈칸에는 '대략'이란 의미의 about이, 두 번째 빈칸에는 '~에 관한'이란 의미의 about이 알맞다 .
9　① on → in ② in → at ④ at → in
10　④ for는 '얼마 동안' 그 일이 계속되었는지를 말할 때 쓰이므로, '언제' 그 일이 일어났는지를 말할 때 쓰이는 전치사 during으로 바꿔야 한다.
11　첫 번째 빈칸에는 시간의 전치사가, 두 번째 빈칸에는 장소의 전치사가 들어가야 한다. by: ~까지(~보다 늦지 않게) next to: ~ 옆에
12　①, ②에는 시간 및 특정 시점을 나타내는 전치사 at이, ③에는 비교적 좁은 장소를 나타내는 전치사 at이 들어가지만, ④에는 특정한 날을 나타내는 전치사 on이 들어간다.
13　without: ~ 없이
14　전치사 across는 '~을 가로질러'의 뜻이므로, through(~을 통과해서)로 고쳐 써야 한다.
15　from과 to는 종종 결합해서 from A to B의 형태로 쓰여, 'A에서 B로', 'A부터 B까지'의 의미를 나타낸다.
16　벤치가 사과나무와 은행나무 사이에 있으므로 전치사 between(~ 사이에)을 쓴다. 강아지가 벤치 아래에 있으므로 under(~ 아래에)를 쓴다. 고양이 두 마리가 벤치 위에 있으므로 on(~ 위에)을 쓴다. 토끼가 사과나무 뒤에 있으므로 behind(~ 뒤에)를 쓴다.

Chapter 04　문장의 형태

Unit 01　주어 + 동사 (+ 주격보어)

CHECK UP　　　　　　　　　p.95

A　1. 1　2. 2　3. 1　4. 2　5. 2　6. 1
B　1. ⓐ　2. ⓑ　3. ⓐ　4. ⓑ

CHECK UP p.97

A
1. some cookies
2. computers
3. a message
4. a sandwich
5. comic books
6. a new cap

B
1. likes steak
2. wants a new phone
3. changed trains
4. eat any meat

LET'S PRACTICE 1 p.98

A
1. ○ 2. ○ 3. X 4. ○ 5. ○ 6. X

B
1. tasty 2. windy 3. bitter 4. well
5. happy

LET'S PRACTICE 2 p.99

A
1. ⓐ 2. ⓐ 3. ⓐ 4. ⓑ 5. ⓐ

B
1. their homework
2. me
3. masks and ropes
4. some cheese
5. more time
6. two slices of ham

STEP UP 1 p.100

A
1. my friends, O
2. interesting, C
3. Korean history, O
4. lonely, C
5. newspapers, O
6. happy, C
7. bread and cakes, O
8. his book, O
9. dark, C
10. famous, C
11. piano, O
12. English, O

B
1. looks cold
2. feels sad
3. gets angry
4. become rich
5. sounds great
6. teaches math
7. walk to school
8. buy clothes
9. love music
10. kept silent

STEP UP 2 p.102

A
1. wear glasses
2. meet him
3. clear the table
4. hit him
5. miss her
6. baking a cake
7. makes dresses
8. posted a notice
9. eating an ice cream
10. like this color
11. bought a new dress
12. wants a new car

B
1. is coming
2. She smiled
3. looks cute
4. smells delicious
5. She arrived
6. tastes good

STEP UP 3 p.104

A
1. dancers were tall
2. He became president
3. looks so perfect
4. This flower smells good
5. The food tasted better
6. looks pretty bad
7. have a good idea
8. he loves soccer
9. He wants a bicycle
10. He changed planes

B
1. The phone rang loudly.
2. He wept for joy.
3. Farmers are very busy these days.
4. She is sick with the flu.
5. The big dog was barking.
6. The train is a half hour late.
7. I ordered the books from a website.
8. Do you ride your motorcycle every day?
9. She studied hard to pass the exam.
10. Add a little more salt and pepper.

STEP UP 4 p.106

A
1. It was hot yesterday.
2. The food was tasty and fresh.
3. This medicine tastes bitter.
4. They study Korean culture.
5. Do you feel better now?
6. My cat can't jump well.
7. I borrowed his pen.
8. They practice soccer on Saturday.
9. The singer became successful.
10. The sky turned red after lunch.

B
1. The man ran quickly to the building.
2. She looks happy today.
3. She studies English on Mondays.
4. Firefighters use heavy equipment.
5. They didn't do this correctly.
6. I met my friend at the airport.
7. A man cleared the snow outside a

house.

8. We walk to school every day.

9. She kept silent during the discussion.

10. I made a mistake on the test.

LEVEL UP
p.108

A
1. became a doctor 2. came late
3. loves me, brother 4. ride your bike
5. ordered a pizza 6. became famous

B
1. is busy 2. It was windy
3. study Korean history
4. borrowed his book
5. is coming 6. barked loudly
7. seems nice 8. changed trains
9. looks beautiful 10. do their homework

Unit 03 주어 + 동사 + 목적어 + 목적어

CHECK UP
p.111

A 1. ⓐ 2. ⓐ 3. ⓑ 4. ⓑ 5. ⓐ

B 1. me 2. me 3. you a cake
4. us English

Unit 04 주어 + 동사 + 목적어 + 목적격 보어

CHECK UP
p.113

A 1. ⓐ 2. ⓐ 3. ⓑ 4. ⓑ 5. ⓑ

B 1. happy 2. wonderful 3. her thirsty
4. short

LET'S PRACTICE 1
p.114

A 1. ⓐ 2. ⓐ 3. ⓑ 4. ⓑ 5. ⓐ

B
1. showed him 2. taught me
3. sent his friend 4. bought me
5. made me 6. tell you

LET'S PRACTICE 2
p.115

A 1. wet. 2. fresh 3. tired 4. attractive
5. boring

B 1. a liar 2. sad 3. quiet 4. guilty
5. wrong 6. crazy

STEP UP 1
p.116

A
1. bought 2. sent 3. showed
4. tell 5. send 6. show
7. makes 8. painted 9. elected
10. named 11. paint

B 1. ⓑ 2. ⓑ 3. ⓐ 4. ⓐ 5. ⓑ 6. ⓑ
7. ⓑ 8. ⓐ 9. ⓑ 10. ⓐ 11. ⓑ

STEP UP 2
p.118

A
1. you something 2. me that
3. you a steak 4. us science
5. him some flowers 6. him a bike
7. her happy 8. the wall yellow
9. Mike captain 10. her son David
11. the soup nice 12. me Julie

B
1. me a present 2. me lunch
3. me an email 4. this box useful
5. me happy 6. my room clean

STEP UP 3
p.120

A
1. bought me a phone
2. sent her a red rose
3. showed me his new phone
4. tell him the truth
5. sent him a message
6. show you my new dress
7. made her happy
8. painted the box red
9. elected him the chairperson
10. named the dog Snoopy

B
1. Mom bought me a backpack.
2. He sent her a sunflower.
3. Mike showed me his new computer.
4. Jane told them the news.
5. I lent him a car.
6. I'll show you my painting.

7. I don't find her attractive.
8. The box keeps the food fresh.
9. It makes me nervous.
10. The snow makes me happy.

STEP UP 4
p.122

A
1. They left the door open.
2. I want to cut my hair short.
3. He bought her a ring.
4. Mom made me a sandwich.
5. I will tell you the truth.
6. The news made us happy.
7. Shopping makes me tired.
8. He found the work interesting.
9. They called him Junhee.
10. They proved him wrong.

B
1. That sound drives me crazy.
2. The movie makes me sleepy.
3. Susan painted her nails red.
4. Did you pay him the money?
   [Did you pay the money to him?]
5. They offered him a good job.
   [They offered a good job to him.]
6. Write him a letter.
   [Write a letter to him.]
7. I want to ask him a question now.
8. Tony finds her new book amazing.
9. Does he keep the room clean?
10. Her friends call her Kitty.

LEVEL UP
p.124

A
1. made, a sweater   2. sent his friend
3. made us wet   4. the work boring
5. sent, an email   6. makes me tired

B
1. sent her some flowers
2. make me happy
3. show you my favorite
4. painted the box purple
5. gave, a present
6. me his plans
7. send him the tickets
8. made her thirsty
9. named their son
10. offered Alex the job

Chapter 04 REVIEW TEST
p.126

1. ① **2.** ② **3.** ① **4.** ③ **5.** ③ **6.** ④ **7.** ③ **8.** ④
9. ④ **10.** ① **11.** ② **12.** ④ **13.** ③
14. nervously → nervous **15.** didn't show him
16. (1) her some flowers (2) gave her (3) happy
(4) gave him

1 동사 taste 다음에 오는 보어로는 형용사인 sweet이 알맞다.

2 Dogs bark는 완전한 문장이므로 동사를 꾸며주는 말로는 부사인 loudly가 알맞다.

3 동사 look 다음에 오는 보어로는 형용사인 beautiful이 알맞다.

4 ① nicely → nice ② tire → tired ④ happily → happy

5 목적어가 필요한 자리이므로 목적격인 them이 알맞다.

6 ④ 「동사 + 목적어」 형태가 알맞으므로 eat any food이 되어야 한다.

7 「be going to meet + 목적어 + 장소 + 시간」의 순서가 알맞으므로, 목적어인 him은 meet 다음에 오는 것이 알맞다.

8 동사 sound의 보어로는 형용사가 알맞으므로 부사인 greatly는 great가 되어야 한다.

9 동사 feel의 보어로는 형용사가 알맞으므로 badly는 bad가 되어야 한다.

10 give, tell 다음에는 「간접목적어(사람) + 직접목적어(사물)」 형태가 이어지므로 빈칸에는 목적격인 me가 오는 것이 알맞다.

11 목적격 보어로는 부사가 아닌 형용사가 알맞으므로 각각 amazing, happy가 들어가야 한다.

12 teach, send, buy, tell 다음에는 전치사 없이 「간접목적어 + 직접목적어」 형태가 이어지는 것이 알맞다.

13 「동사(made) + 목적어(목적격: her) + 목적격 보어(형용사: sad)의 형태」가 오는 것이 알맞다.

14 목적격 보어로는 부사가 아닌 형용사가 알맞으므로 nervously는 nervous가 되어야 한다.

15 '보여주지 않았다'는 didn't show로 쓰고, 이어서 간접목적어인 him을 넣는 것이 알맞다.

16 (1), (2), (4) 「주어 + 동사 + 간접목적어(사람) + 직접목적어(사물)」의 형태가 알맞다.
(3) 「주어 + 동사 + 목적어 + 목적격 보어(형용사)」의 형태가 알맞다.

실전 Test 02회
p.130

1. ② **2.** ③ **3.** ② **4.** ④ **5.** ③ **6.** ② **7.** ④ **8.** ④
9. ② **10.** ① **11.** ① **12.** ① **13.** ④ **14.** ① **15.** ②
16. ② **17.** ④ **18.** ④ **19.** He will learn how to skate during the vacation. **20.** for → from
21. made me **22.** show, next to, bought, sang, tasty, happy

1   ①, ③, ④의 about은 '~에 관해'라는 의미의 전치사이고, ②의 about은 '대략'이라는 의미의 전치사이다.

2   장소의 전치사 in은 the park 앞에 오는 것이 알맞다.

3   next to: ~ 옆에

4   '~ 동안'을 뜻하면서 그 일이 언제 일어났는지를 말할 때 쓰이는 전치사는 during이다.

5   전치사 on은 장소를 나타낼 때는 '~ 위에'라는 뜻으로, 특정한 날을 나타낼 때는 '~에'라는 뜻으로 쓰인다.

6   give, show 다음에는 「간접목적어(사람) + 직접목적어(사물)」 형태가 이어지므로 빈칸에는 목적격인 me가 오는 것이 알맞다.

7   ④ 전치사 뒤에 대명사가 올 때는 반드시 목적격을 쓴다. they → them

8   ① tire → tired ② nicely → nice ③ happily → happy

9   두 번째 빈칸에 '~까지, ~보다 늦지 않게'를 나타내는 전치사 by가 들어가야 하므로, 첫 번째 빈칸에는 in front of가 오는 것을 알 수 있다.

10 목적격 보어로는 부사가 아닌 형용사가 알맞으므로 각각 clear, happy가 들어가야 한다.

11 ②, ③, ④의 빈칸에는 날짜나 요일, 특정한 날을 가리키는 전치사 on이 들어가지만, ①의 빈칸에는 기간을 나타내는 전치사 for가 들어가야 한다.

12 give, teach, send, buy 다음에는 「간접목적어 + 직접목적어」 형태가 이어지는 것이 알맞다.

13 '~ 없이'를 뜻하는 전치사는 without이다.

14 「동사(made) + 목적어(목적격: us) + 목적격 보어(형용사: sad)」의 형태가 오는 것이 알맞다.

15 주어진 문장과 ①, ③, ④의 in은 장소를 나타내는 전치사이지만, ②의 in은 시간을 나타내는 전치사이다.

16 목적어가 필요한 자리이므로 목적격인 them이 알맞다.

17 동사 feel의 보어로는 형용사가 알맞으므로 greatly는 great이 되어야 한다.

18 동사 look의 보어로는 형용사가 알맞으므로 beautifully는 beautiful이 되어야 한다.

19 그는 배울 것이다(He will learn) + 스케이트 타는 법을 (how to skate) + 방학 동안(during the vacation)의 순서로 배열하는 것이 가장 적절하다.

20 from(+ 출발지)과 to(+ 도착지)는 종종 결합해서 from A to B의 형태로 쓰여, 'A에서 B로', 'A부터 B까지'의 의미를 나타낸다.

21 '만들어 주셨다'는 make의 과거형 made로 쓰고, 이어서 간접목적어인 me를 넣는 것이 알맞다.

22 show, buy, sing 등의 동사 뒤에는 두 개의 목적어가 쓰이며, '(누구에게 무엇을) 해주다'라는 뜻을 갖고 있다. 동사 make가 쓰인 문장은 목적어가 어떤 상태인지를 설명하기 위해 「주어 + 동사 + 목적어 + 목적격 보어」 형태가 될 수 있으며, 목적격 보어로 형용사가 자주 쓰인다. next to: ~ 옆에

총괄평가 01회

1. ③ **2.** ① **3.** ③ **4.** ⑤ **5.** ② **6.** ④ **7.** ⑤ **8.** ③
9. ② **10.** ① **11.** ③ **12.** ④ **13.** ② **14.** ③ **15.** ⑤
16. about **17.** famously → famous **18.** It was windy last night. **19.** I want to paint my room blue. **20.** playing

총괄평가 02회

1. ② **2.** ② **3.** ② **4.** ⑤ **5.** ③ **6.** ③ **7.** ⑤ **8.** ④
9. ① **10.** ② **11.** ④ **12.** ⑤ **13.** ③ **14.** ③ **15.** ④
16. until **17.** sadly → sad **18.** Time proved them wrong. **19.** Sunlight comes in through the hole. **20.** to hurt

초등 Grammar Inside

Workbook Answer Key

6

Unit 01 - 02

WORD PRACTICE 2 p.4

A
1. plan 2. Internet 3. join
4. collect 5. leave 6. promise

B
1. solve 2. spend 3. expect
4. practices 5. found

C
1. fix 2. forget 3. weight
4. bake 5. switch 6. fireworks

GRAMMAR PRACTICE 1 p.6

A
1. To sing, ⓐ 2. to tell, ⓐ
3. to have, ⓑ 4. to fly, ⓒ
5. to be, ⓒ

B
1. to study 2. to play 3. to go
4. to eat 5. to spend 6. to become

C
1. ○ 2. to travel[traveling] 3. to collect
[collecting] 4. ○ 5. ○ 6. to study 7. ○
8. to read 9. ○ 10. ○ 11. to play
12. to swim

GRAMMAR PRACTICE 2 p.8

A
1. to cry 2. to arrive 3. to buy 4. to open
5. to answer 6. to go 7. to ride 8. to see
9. to drink 10. to give

B
1. something to drink
2. to take a break
3. to speak English
4. to bake a cake

5. stopped to look at
6. to see animals
7. time to travel
8. to help me

GRAMMAR PRACTICE 3 p.10

A
1. I went there to fix my computer.
2. I want to go to the park.
3. I got up early to do my homework.
4. She ran home to get her book.
5. It's time to close the shop.
6. I started to read the novel yesterday.
7. His goal is to lose weight.
8. Do you want to buy a new smartphone?
9. I studied hard to get a good mark.
10. She practices hard to speak English well.

B
1. I took a taxi to arrive on time.
2. I have something to tell you.
3. He learned to drive when he was 17.
4. I'm saving money to buy a new bike.
5. His hope is to be a singer.
6. I have some money to spend.
7. I hope to visit Canada someday.
8. Follow these steps to download the apps.
9. I went to the kitchen to get some salt.
10. It is wrong to hurt animals.

GRAMMAR PRACTICE 4 p.12

A
1. to catch
2. to turn off
3. time to waste
4. to visit
5. to play soccer
6. something to eat
7. to hurt animals
8. money to go
9. easy to solve
10. expect to see
11. to help me
12. Her wish is to visit the White House.
13. He ran to catch the bus.
14. He forgot to turn off the light.
15. We have no time to rest.
16. I need something to drink.
17. I went there to play basketball.

Unit 01 - 02

WORD PRACTICE 2 p.16

A
1. fishing 2. prize 3. forest
4. bathroom 5. headache 6. shout

B
1. quit 2. mind 3. wish
4. decided 5. explaining

C

r	m	s	e	a	r	e	m	s	c
s	j	e	x	e	r	c	i	s	e
c	h	o	c	s	o	w	s	a	t
y	u	z	h	i	g	h	t	k	l
c	l	e	a	n	r	t	a	e	o
l	t	b	n	i	o	g	k	p	e
e	s	n	g	r	o	w	e	e	y
v	s	x	e	y	e	d	t	r	n

1. mistake 2. cycle 3. grow
4. exercise 5. clean 6. exchange

GRAMMAR PRACTICE 1 p.18

A
1. Skiing, ⓐ 2. cycling, ⓑ
3. playing, ⓒ 4. jumping, ⓒ
5. doing, ⓑ

B
1. smoking 2. to succeed 3. making
4. to go 5. running 6. to come

C
1. ○ 2. walking 3. ○ 4. to go
5. ○ 6. ○ 7. making 8. to go
9. to see 10. to grow 11. trying 12. ○

GRAMMAR PRACTICE 2 p.20

A
1. running 2. playing 3. turning
4. going 5. to stay 6. jogging
7. to leave 8. skiing 9. trying
10. reading

B
1. to eat 2. swimming 3. to visit
4. crying 5. working 6. explaining
7. doing 8. to drink 9. to go
10. washing 11. meeting 12. to arrive

GRAMMAR PRACTICE 3 p.22

A
1. finish reading this book
2. mind turning down the music
3. needs to lose
4. gave up teaching
5. stopped writing
6. enjoy meeting, seeing
7. keeps trying to talk
8. avoids talking
9. wish to visit you
10. planning to stay

B
1. He hates making[to make] mistakes.
2. I don't mind waiting.
3. I need to go to the bathroom.
4. Katie chose to stay away from work that day.
5. He enjoys watching birds.
6. Stop talking and listen!
7. She needs to feel loved.
8. I was hoping to leave work early today.
9. I hate leaving[to leave] home.
10. He needs to lose some weight.

GRAMMAR PRACTICE 4 p.24

A
1. want to be
2. go swimming
3. finished doing the dishes
4. wishes to see
5. promised to come
6. you mind exchanging
7. started to run
8. enjoys walking
9. hate waiting for
10. decided to grow
11. plan to go
12. I finished doing my homework.
13. I go hiking once a week.
14. I hate waiting[to wait] for the bus.
15. Would you mind opening the window?
16. I enjoy playing basketball.
17. He wishes to meet you.

Chapter 03 전치사

Unit 01 - 02

WORD PRACTICE 2   p.28

A
1. clap   2. hunter   3. market
4. church   5. tower   6. vacation

B
1. bank   2. hill   3. rock   4. vase   5. history

C

r	m	c	c	l	g	w	e	s	c
s	f	r	h	w	y	b	w	a	y
c	p	y	r	a	m	i	d	a	t
o	i	w	e	l	e	h	l	k	l
u	l	s	o	l	d	i	e	r	o
c	l	e	v	e	r	g	e	p	e
q	o	p	o	t	a	t	o	e	y
v	w	u	r	s	e	w	t	r	n

1. gym   2. wallet   3. pyramid
4. potato   5. soldier   6. pillow

GRAMMAR PRACTICE 1   p.30

A
1. at   2. at   3. on   4. in   5. on   6. in
7. in   8. at   9. in   10. at

B
1. during   2. by   3. until   4. for

C
1. X   2. ○   3. ○   4. ○   5. X   6. ○
7. X   8. X   9. ○   10. X   11. X   12. ○

GRAMMAR PRACTICE 2   p.32

A
1. in   2. on   3. during   4. At   5. at
6. in   7. in   8. in   9. during   10. behind
11. in front of   12. until

B
1. on Friday
2. by nine
3. on the bench
4. at 6 o'clock
5. in the cage
6. between the trees
7. for a week
8. on my birthday

GRAMMAR PRACTICE 3   p.34

A
1. in the sea
2. until the weekend
3. in front of the hospital
4. during the summer
5. behind the sofa
6. on the roof
7. behind the building
8. on Saturday
9. in 2017
10. next to the gym

B
1. My bike is in front of the bookstore.
2. A river flows between the two mountains.
3. I visited my grandmother on New Year's Day.
4. I will finish the homework by Thursday.
5. The post office is next to the library.
6. It rained a lot during the morning.
7. They arrived late at the airport.
8. The museum closes at 5 p.m.
9. A bird is sitting on your hat.
10. I'm going to study math until 5 p.m.

GRAMMAR PRACTICE 4   p.36

A
1. on her birthday
2. during the break
3. under the desk
4. in the afternoon
5. at the bus stop
6. at breakfast
7. behind the monitor
8. next to, rock
9. between, two islands
10. under the table
11. in the summer
12. They drink milk at night.
13. The backpack is on the chair.
14. He read magazines during the day.
15. A lion is sitting in front of a rock.
16. They go to the mountains in the winter.
17. There is a fly behind the monitor.

WORD PRACTICE 2   p.40

A   1. desert   2. tunnel   3. glasses
     4. pumpkin   5. butterfly   6. mosquito

B   1. flying   2. stairs   3. hole
     4. bubbles   5. village

C

c	b	q	a	c	h	g	w	e	s
y	s	e	b	a	k	e	r	y	a
t	c	l	a	d	d	e	r	e	a
p	e	g	l	r	o	c	o	t	k
e	a	g	l	e	u	d	o	l	e
a	r	l	o	e	x	q	f	d	h
r	t	r	o	n	g	e	n	a	e
n	h	n	n	r	s	n	w	t	r

   1. bakery   2. ladder   3. eagle
   4. pear   5. roof   6. balloon

GRAMMAR PRACTICE 1   p.42

A   1. to   2. through   3. about   4. without
     5. by   6. across   7. down   8. about

B   1. up   2. with   3. down   4. without

C   1. ○   2. ○   3. X   4. X   5. ○   6. ○
     7. X   8. X   9. ○   10. X   11. X   12. ○

GRAMMAR PRACTICE 2   p.44

A   1. like   2. by   3. with
     4. without   5. through   6. up
     7. to   8. across   9. down

B   1. with her family
     2. by bicycle
     3. through the village
     4. across the road
     5. about Korean history
     6. on foot
     7. without a mask
     8. like a horse

GRAMMAR PRACTICE 3   p.46

A   1. falling down
     2. across the playground
     3. like an orange
     4. about a cat
     5. through the hole
     6. from the tree
     7. up the hill
     8. by ship
     9. with his friends
     10. like a pumpkin

B   1. Don't go camping without me.
     2. A bee came in through the window.
     3. Butterflies fly from flower to flower.
     4. A starfish looks like a star.
     5. Look at the girl with blond hair.
     6. An iguana is climbing up the wall.
     7. My family will go to the zoo.
     8. He ran across the square.
     9. A balloon is coming down to the ground.
     10. The baby smiles like an angel.

GRAMMAR PRACTICE 4   p.48

A   1. by taxi
     2. about two hours
     3. like an elephant
     4. without his parents
     5. through the forest
     6. from, diving board
     7. to the ground
     8. across the room
     9. about animals
     10. to the post office
     11. with the long tail
     12. He went to the hospital without his
        parents.
     13. The rock looks like a lion.
     14. He slept for about an hour.
     15. A child[kid] is walking across the street.
     16. I want to go home by bus.
     17. I read a book about cats and dogs.

Chapter 04 문장의 형태

Unit 01 - 02

WORD PRACTICE 2   p.52

A 1. bark 2. cinema 3. loudly
4. company 5. website 6. lonely

B 1. Add 2. culture 3. borrowed 4. cleared
5. posted

C

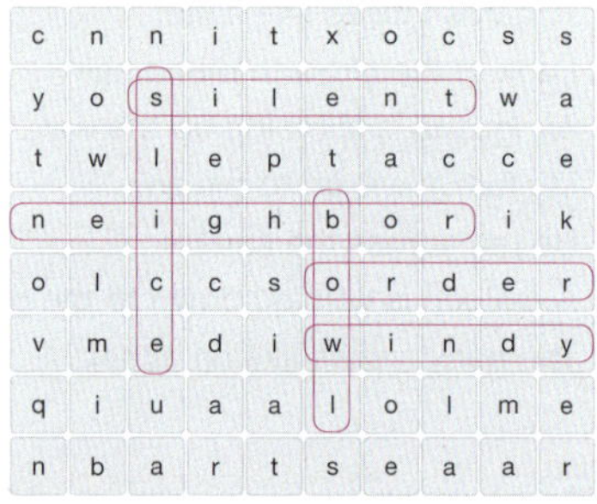

1. neighbor 2. silent 3. order
4. slice 5. windy 6. bowl

GRAMMAR PRACTICE 1   p.54

A 1. ○ 2. X 3. X 4. ○ 5. ○ 6. X 7. X
8. ○ 9. X 10. ○

B 1. ⓐ 2. ⓐ 3. ⓑ 4. ⓑ 5. ⓐ 6. ⓐ
7. ⓐ

GRAMMAR PRACTICE 2   p.56

A 1. nice 2. good 3. great
4. baked 5. eating 6. likes
7. makes 8. posted 9. bought
10. wants 11. changed 12. eat

B 1. is tall 2. became 3. is working
4. likes 5. rang 6. busy
7. late 8. ordered 9. ride
10. me 11. Add 12. miss

GRAMMAR PRACTICE 3   p.58

A 1. well 2. interesting 3. lonely
4. great[good] 5. cute 6. good[great]
7. better 8. bad 9. late
10. bitter

B 1. She was sick.
2. He wants a bicycle for his birthday.
3. You look happy today.
4. That person gets angry very easily.
5. We all want to become rich, right?
6. Why do we love music?
7. I wear glasses for reading.
8. She hit him hard.
9. I bought a new dress yesterday.
10. I borrowed his book yesterday.

GRAMMAR PRACTICE 4   p.60

A 1. borrowed his pen
2. didn't do that
3. tasty and fresh
4. He changed planes
5. She studied hard
6. you feel better
7. turned red
8. like this color
9. need more time
10. made a mistake
11. It was hot
12. I borrowed his book.
13. The food was cold and dry.
14. Do you like this movie?
15. Do you need more time?
16. He changed trains.
17. It was cold yesterday.

Unit 03 - 04

WORD PRACTICE 2   p.62

A 1. lend 2. garlic 3. offer
4. spinach 5. nail 6. chairman

B 1. send 2. attractive 3. thirsty
4. awful 5. favorite

C

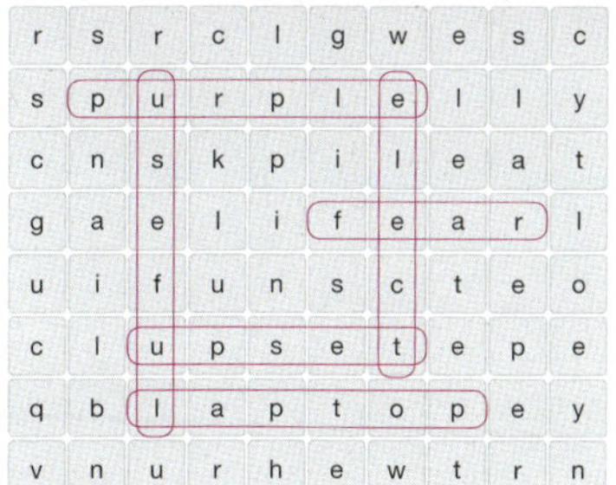

1. purple   2. laptop   3. upset
4. elect   5. useful   6. fear

GRAMMAR PRACTICE 1   p.66

A   1. ○   2. X   3. X   4. ○   5. ○   6. X
7. X   8. ○   9. X   10. ○

B   1. ⓐ   2. ⓐ   3. ⓑ   4. ⓑ   5. ⓐ   6. ⓐ
7. ⓐ

GRAMMAR PRACTICE 2   p.68

A   1. sent   2. show   3. happy
4. Mike chairman   5. her   6. upset
7. nervous   8. you   9. us science
10. me   11. fresh   12. attractive

B   1. him her pictures
2. his friend a gift
3. made her sad
4. kept them quiet
5. her friend a liar
6. found the work interesting
7. proved them wrong
8. tell you the story
9. drive me crazy
10. taught me English
11. the box purple
12. their son John

GRAMMAR PRACTICE 3   p.70

A   1. bought   2. made   3. showed
4. paint   5. send   6. call
7. told   8. elected   9. finds
10. keep

B   1. Please send him the tickets.
2. She bought him a bike for Christmas.

3. Mom gave me a present.
4. Music makes me happy.
5. I don't find her attractive.
6. It makes me nervous.
7. They left the door open.
8. Shopping makes me tired.
9. They proved him wrong.
10. Tony finds her new book amazing.

GRAMMAR PRACTICE 4   p.72

A   1. pay her
2. show him
3. makes her happy
4. named her son
5. bought me lunch
6. sent me an email
7. call her Kitty
8. keep the room clean
9. ask him a question
10. offered him a good job
11. makes me sleepy
12. I want to ask her a favor now.
13. I didn't show him the message.
14. Tony bought me a pen.
15. Jane named her daughter Amy.
16. He sent me a gift.
17. The movie makes me happy.

MEMO

MEMO

MEMO

MEMO

MEMO

초등
Grammar
Inside

Answer Key

NE능률 교재 MAP

아래 교재 MAP을 참고하여 본인의 현재 혹은 목표 수준에 따라 교재를 선택하세요.
NE능률 교재들과 함께 영어실력을 쑥쑥~ 올려보세요!
MP3 등 교재 부가 학습 서비스 및 자세한 교재 정보는 www.nebooks.co.kr 에서 확인하세요.

초1-2	초3	초3-4	초4-5	초5-6
	그래머버디 1	그래머버디 2	그래머버디 3	Grammar Bean 3
	초등영어 문법이 된다 Starter 1	초등 Grammar Inside 1	Grammar Bean 1	Grammar Bean 4
		초등 Grammar Inside 2	Grammar Bean 2	초등영어 문법이 된다 2
			초등영어 문법이 된다 1	초등 Grammar Inside 5
			초등 Grammar Inside 3	초등 Grammar Inside 6
			초등 Grammar Inside 4	

초6-예비중	중1	중1-2	중2-3	중3
능률중학영어 예비중	능률중학영어 중1	능률중학영어 중2	Grammar Zone 기초편	능률중학영어 중3
Grammar Inside Starter	Grammar Zone 입문편	1316팬클럽 문법 2	Grammar Zone 워크북 기초편	1316팬클럽 문법 3
원리를 더한 영문법 STARTER	Grammar Zone 워크북 입문편	문제로 마스터하는 중학영문법 2	고득점 독해를 위한 중학 구문 마스터 2	문제로 마스터하는 중학영문법 3
	1316팬클럽 문법 1	Grammar Inside 2	원리를 더한 영문법 2	Grammar Inside 3
	문제로 마스터하는 중학영문법 1	열중 16강 문법 2	중학영문법 총정리 모의고사 2	열중 16강 문법 3
	Grammar Inside 1	고득점 독해를 위한 중학 구문 마스터 1	쓰기로 마스터하는 중학서술형 2학년	고득점 독해를 위한 중학 구문 마스터 3
	열중 16강 문법 1	원리를 더한 영문법 1	천문장 입문	중학영문법 총정리 모의고사 3
	쓰기로 마스터하는 중학서술형 1학년	중학영문법 총정리 모의고사 1		쓰기로 마스터하는 중학서술형 3학년

예비고-고1	고1	고1-2	고2-3	고3
문제로 마스터하는 고등영문법	Grammar Zone 기본편 1	필히 통하는 고등영문법 실력편	Grammar Zone 종합편	
올클 수능 어법 start	Grammar Zone 워크북 기본편 1	TEPS BY STEP G+R Basic	Grammar Zone 워크북 종합편	
천문장 기본	Grammar Zone 기본편 2		올클 수능 어법 완성	
	Grammar Zone 워크북 기본편 2		천문장 완성	
	필히 통하는 고등영문법 기본			

수능 이상 / 토플 80-89 · 텝스 600-699점	수능 이상 / 토플 90-99 · 텝스 700-799점	수능 이상 / 토플 100 · 텝스 800점 이상		
TEPS BY STEP G+R 1	TEPS BY STEP G+R 2	TEPS BY STEP G+R 3		

초등
Grammar Inside

Workbook

6

초등

Grammar

Inside

Workbook

6

A 다음 단어를 두 번씩 듣고 따라 쓴 후 그 뜻을 쓰세요.

단어	두 번 따라 쓰기		뜻 쓰기
travel 여행하다			
job 일, 직업			
spend (돈을) 쓰다			
practice 연습하다			
save 저축하다			
find 찾다			
plan 계획			
leave 떠나다			
fireworks 불꽃놀이			
join 가입하다			
wish 소망			
collect 모으다			
cellphone 휴대전화			

단어	두 번 따라 쓰기	뜻 쓰기
bake 굽다		
forget 잊다		
expect 기대하다		
promise 약속, 약속하다		
Internet 인터넷		
lose 지다, 줄이다		
weight 체중, 무게		
fix 수리하다		
follow 따라가다		
step 단계		
firefighter 소방관		
switch 스위치		
solve 풀다, 해결하다		

A 주어진 철자의 순서를 바르게 맞추어 우리말 뜻에 해당하는 단어를 쓰세요.

1 
lpan
계획

2 
lntreent
인터넷

3 
inoj
가입하다

4 
eclloct
모으다

5 
levea
떠나다

6 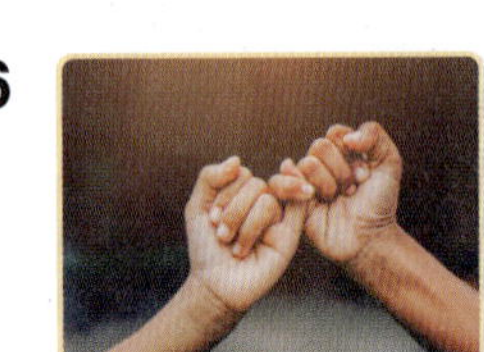
rosepmi
약속, 약속하다

B 우리말과 같은 뜻이 되도록 보기 에서 알맞은 단어를 골라 쓰세요.

보기　practices　found　spend　expect　solve

1 It is easy to _______________ the problem.　그 문제를 푸는 것은 쉽다.

2 I have no money to _______________.　나는 쓸 돈이 없다.

3 I didn't _______________ to see you here.　내가 여기서 너를 보리라고는 생각하지 못했다.

4 She _______________ hard to speak English well.
그녀는 영어를 잘하기 위해 열심히 연습한다.

5 I _______________ a good place to study.　나는 공부하기에 좋은 장소를 찾았다.

C 다음 사진에 해당하는 단어를 아래 퍼즐에서 찾아 ○ 표시하고 빈칸에 쓰세요.

m	n	g	l	o	w	e	p	c	r
j	c	w	e	r	t	e	c	b	s
w	i	e	t	o	w	f	t	a	p
u	f	i	r	e	w	o	r	k	s
f	i	g	c	h	w	r	f	e	u
t	x	h	i	x	g	g	p	e	z
s	n	t	l	o	w	e	e	y	q
i	k	f	s	w	i	t	c	h	v

1 

수리하다

2 

잊다

3 

체중, 무게

4 

굽다

5 

스위치

6 

불꽃놀이

A to부정사에 밑줄을 긋고, 문장에서의 역할을 고르세요.

1 To sing is fun.
노래를 하는 것은 재미있다.
ⓐ 주어　ⓑ 목적어　ⓒ 보어

2 It is wrong to tell a lie.
거짓말을 하는 것은 잘못이다.
ⓐ 주어　ⓑ 목적어　ⓒ 보어

3 I want to have a hamburger.
나는 햄버거가 먹고 싶다.
ⓐ 주어　ⓑ 목적어　ⓒ 보어

4 Her dream is to fly.
그녀의 꿈은 하늘을 나는 것이다.
ⓐ 주어　ⓑ 목적어　ⓒ 보어

5 Her goal is to be a pilot.
그녀의 목표는 조종사가 되는 것이다.
ⓐ 주어　ⓑ 목적어　ⓒ 보어

B (　) 안에서 알맞은 것을 고르세요.

1 It's time (study / to study).
공부할 시간이다.

2 His hobby is (play / to play) computer games.
그의 취미는 컴퓨터 게임을 하는 것이다.

3 I want (to go / going) to the soccer field.
나는 축구장에 가고 싶다.

4 Do you want something (to eat / eating)?
너는 뭔가 먹고 싶니?

5 I have no money (spending / to spend).
나는 쓸 돈이 없다.

6 Tom practices hard (become / to become) a soccer player.
Tom은 축구 선수가 되기 위해 열심히 연습한다.

C 밑줄 친 부분이 맞으면 ○ 표시하고, 틀리면 바르게 고쳐 쓰세요.

1 I need some water to drink.
나는 마실 물이 좀 필요하다.

2 I like travel with my friends.
나는 친구들과 여행하는 것을 좋아한다.

3 His hobby is to be collect toy cars.
그의 취미는 장난감 차를 모으는 것이다.

4 I went out to watch a movie.
나는 영화를 보러 나갔다.

5 This is the best time to start.
지금이 시작하기에 가장 좋은 시간이다.

6 She will go to New York studying English.
그녀는 영어를 공부하기 위해 뉴욕에 갈 것이다.

7 It is fun to swim in the sea.
바다에서 수영하는 것은 재미있다.

8 She gave me a book reading.
그녀는 나에게 읽을 책을 주었다.

9 Karen ran to avoid being late.
Karen은 늦지 않으려고 달렸다.

10 He saves money to travel.
그는 여행을 하기 위해 돈을 모은다.

11 I went there playing baseball with my friends.
나는 내 친구들과 야구를 하기 위해 거기에 갔다.

12 It is dangerous swim in the river.
강에서 수영하는 것은 위험하다.

A 우리말과 같은 뜻이 되도록 보기 에서 알맞은 단어를 골라 to부정사로 바꿔 쓰세요.

> 보기   answer   arrive   buy   cry   drink
>   open   give   go   ride   see

1 The girl started ____________________.
그 소녀는 울기 시작했다.

2 I took the subway ____________________ on time.
나는 제시간에 도착하기 위해 지하철을 탔다.

3 He saved money ____________________ a computer.
그는 컴퓨터를 살 돈을 모았다.

4 Do you know the number ____________________ the door?
너는 문을 열 번호를 알고 있니?

5 I have an email ____________________.
나는 답장을 해야 할 이메일이 있다.

6 I decided not ____________________ there.
나는 거기에 가지 않기로 결정했다.

7 Jane learned ____________________ a bike.
Jane은 자전거 타기를 배웠다.

8 It is exciting ____________________ fireworks.
불꽃놀이를 보는 것은 신난다.

9 I went to the kitchen ____________________ some water.
나는 물을 좀 마시러 부엌에 갔다.

10 He bought some flowers ____________________ to his sister.
그는 여동생에게 줄 꽃을 좀 샀다.

B 우리말과 같은 뜻이 되도록 주어진 말을 이용하여 빈칸에 알맞은 말을 쓰세요.

1 뭘 좀 마시고 싶니? (something, drink)

→ Would you like ______________ ______________ ______________?

2 쉴 시간이다. (a break, take)

→ It's time ______________ ______________ ______________ ______________.

3 영어를 말하는 것은 어렵지 않다. (English, speak)

→ It's not difficult ______________ ______________ ______________.

4 케이크를 굽는 것은 쉽다. (bake, a cake)

→ It is easy ______________ ______________ ______________ ______________.

5 우리는 그 그림을 보기 위해 멈추어 섰다. (stop, look at)

→ We ______________ ______________ ______________ ______________ the painting.

6 그늘은 동물들을 보려고 동물원에 갈 것이다. (see, animals)

→ They will go to the zoo ______________ ______________ ______________.

7 나는 여행할 시간이 없다. (travel, time)

→ I don't have ______________ ______________ ______________.

8 그는 나를 돕겠다고 약속했다. (help)

→ He made a promise ______________ ______________ ______________.

A (   ) 안의 말을 알맞은 곳에 넣어 문장을 완성하세요.

1 I went there my computer. (to fix)   나는 내 컴퓨터를 고치기 위해 거기에 갔다.

→ ____

2 I want to the park. (to go)   나는 공원에 가고 싶다.

→ ____

3 I got up early my homework. (to do)   나는 숙제를 하기 위해 일찍 일어났다.

→ ____

4 She ran home her book. (to get)   그녀는 자신의 책을 가지러 집으로 달려갔다.

→ ____

5 It's time the shop. (to close)   가게를 닫을 시간이다.

→ ____

6 I started the novel yesterday. (to read)   나는 그 소설을 어제 읽기 시작했다.

→ ____

7 His goal is weight. (to lose)   그의 목표는 몸무게를 줄이는 것이다.

→ ____

8 Do you want a new smartphone? (to buy)   너는 새 스마트폰을 사고 싶니?

→ ____

9 I studied hard a good mark. (to get)   나는 좋은 점수를 얻기 위해 열심히 공부했다.

→ ____

10 She practices hard English well. (to speak)   그녀는 영어를 잘하기 위해 열심히 연습한다.

→ ____

B 밑줄 친 부분을 바르게 고쳐 문장을 다시 쓰세요.

1 I took a taxi on time to arrive.   나는 제시간에 도착하려고 택시를 탔다.

➡ ____

2 I have something tell you.   나는 너에게 할 말이 있다.

➡ ____

3 He learned to driving when he was 17.   그는 열일곱 살에 운전을 배웠다.

➡ ____

4 I'm saving money a new bike to buy.   나는 새 자전거를 사기 위해 돈을 저축하고 있다.

➡ ____

5 His hope is a singer to be.   그의 희망은 가수가 되는 것이다.

➡ ____

6 I have to spend some money.   나는 쓸 돈이 좀 있다.

➡ ____

7 I hope visit Canada someday.   나는 언젠가 캐나다를 방문하고 싶다.

➡ ____

8 Follow these steps downloading the apps.   앱을 다운 받으려면 이 단계들을 따르세요.

➡ ____

9 I went to get some salt to the kitchen.   나는 소금을 좀 가지러 부엌에 갔다.

➡ ____

10 It is to hurt animals wrong.   동물을 해치는 것은 잘못이다.

➡ ____

A 우리말과 같은 뜻이 되도록 주어진 말을 이용하여 문장을 완성하세요.

1 그는 기차를 타려고 달렸다. (catch)

➜ He ran ______________ ______________ the train.

2 그는 스위치를 끄는 것을 잊었다. (turn off)

➜ He forgot ______________ ______________ ______________ the switch.

3 우리는 낭비할 시간이 없다. (time, waste)

➜ We have no ______________ ______________ ______________.

4 그의 소망은 청와대를 방문하는 것이다. (visit)

➜ His wish is ______________ ______________ the Blue House.

5 나는 거기에 축구하러 갔다. (play soccer)

➜ I went there ______________ ______________ ______________.

6 나는 먹을 게 필요하다. (something, eat)

➜ I need ______________ ______________ ______________.

7 동물을 해치는 것은 잘못이다. (hurt, animals)

➜ It is wrong ______________ ______________ ______________.

8 그는 런던에 가려고 돈을 모으고 있다. (money, go)

➜ He is saving ______________ ______________ ______________ to London.

9   그 문제를 푸는 것은 쉽다. (easy, solve)

→ It is ______________ ______________ ______________ the problem.

10   우리는 서로 만나리라고 기대하지 않았다. (expect, see)

→ We didn't ______________ ______________ ______________ each other.

11   나는 나를 도와줄 친구가 있다. (help)

→ I have a friend ______________ ______________ ______________.

12   그녀의 소망은 백악관을 방문하는 것이다. (the White House)

→ ____

13   그는 버스를 타려고 달렸다. (catch)

→ ____

14   그는 불을 끄는 것을 잊었다. (the light)

→ ____

15   우리는 쉴 시간이 없다. (no time, rest)

→ ____

16   나는 마실 게 필요하다. (drink)

→ ____

17   나는 거기에 농구하러 갔다. (basketball)

→ ____

A 다음 단어를 두 번씩 듣고 따라 쓴 후 그 뜻을 쓰세요.

단어	두 번 따라 쓰기	뜻 쓰기
cycle 자전거를 타다		
ski 스키		
snowman 눈사람		
clean 청소하다		
believe 믿다		
daily 매일의		
exercise 운동하다		
quit 그만두다		
mind 꺼리다		
do the dishes 설거지하다		
exchange 교환하다		
wish 바라다		
decide 결정하다		

단어	두 번 따라 쓰기		뜻 쓰기
fishing 낚시			
grow 기르다			
prize 상, 상품			
forest 숲			
asleep 잠이 든			
bathroom 화장실			
jog 조깅하다			
shout 소리치다			
volume 음량			
headache 두통			
explain 설명하다			
sandwich 샌드위치			
mistake 실수			

A 주어진 철자의 순서를 바르게 맞추어 우리말 뜻에 해당하는 단어를 쓰세요.

1 
fisghin
낚시

2
ripez
상, 상품

3 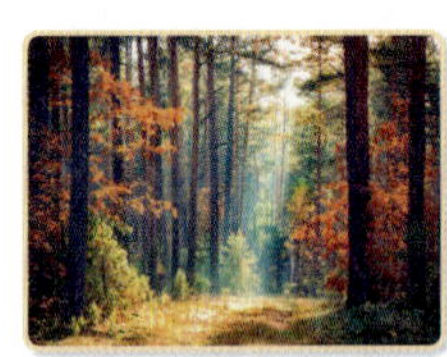
orstfe
숲

4
baroomth
화장실

5 
achheade
두통

6 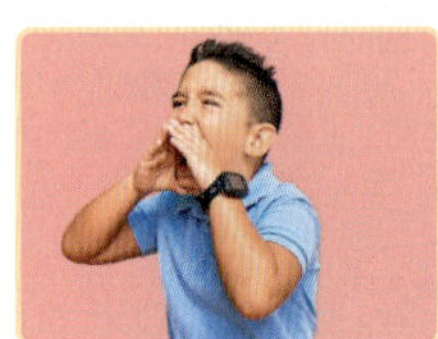
toush
소리치다

B 우리말과 같은 뜻이 되도록 보기 에서 알맞은 단어를 골라 쓰세요.

보기   decided   explaining   mind   quit   wish

1 My dad ________________ smoking.   아빠는 담배를 끊으셨다.

2 Do you ________________ turning down the music?   음악 소리 좀 낮춰 줄래요?

3 I ________________ to see you again.   다음에 또 볼 수 있으면 좋겠습니다.

4 She ________________ to grow her hair.   그녀는 머리를 기르기로 결정했다.

5 Would you mind ________________ that again?   그거 다시 한 번 설명해 주시겠어요?

C 다음 사진에 해당하는 단어를 아래 퍼즐에서 찾아 ○ 표시하고 빈칸에 쓰세요.

r	m	s	e	a	r	e	m	s	c
s	j	e	x	e	r	c	i	s	e
c	h	o	c	s	o	w	s	a	t
y	u	z	h	i	g	h	t	k	l
c	l	e	a	n	r	t	a	e	o
l	t	b	n	i	o	g	k	p	e
e	s	n	g	r	o	w	e	e	y
v	s	x	e	y	e	d	t	r	n

1

실수

2

자전거를 타다

3

기르다

4

운동하다

5

청소하다

6

교환하다

A　동명사에 밑줄을 긋고, 문장에서의 역할을 고르세요.

1　Skiing is difficult.
스키를 타는 것은 어렵다.
ⓐ 주어　ⓑ 목적어　ⓒ 보어

2　I hate cycling.
나는 자전거 타기를 싫어한다.
ⓐ 주어　ⓑ 목적어　ⓒ 보어

3　His hobby is playing tennis.
그의 취미는 테니스를 치는 것이다.
ⓐ 주어　ⓑ 목적어　ⓒ 보어

4　My cat's favorite activity is jumping.
내 고양이가 가장 좋아하는 활동은 뛰어오르기이다.
ⓐ 주어　ⓑ 목적어　ⓒ 보어

5　She finished doing the dishes.
그녀는 설거지를 끝냈다.
ⓐ 주어　ⓑ 목적어　ⓒ 보어

B　( ) 안에서 알맞은 것을 고르세요.

1　Dad gave up (to smoke / smoking).
아빠는 담배를 끊으셨다.

2　They hope (to succeed / succeeding).
그들은 성공하기를 희망한다.

3　He avoids (to make / making) a decision.
그는 결정을 내리는 것을 피한다.

4　I want (going / to go) to the soccer field.
나는 축구장에 가고싶다.

5　She enjoys (to run / running) daily.
그녀는 매일 달리기 하는 것을 즐긴다.

6　He promised (to come / coming) back.
그는 돌아오겠다고 약속했다.

C 밑줄 친 부분이 맞으면 ○ 표시하고, 틀리면 바르게 고쳐 쓰세요.

1 Running is good for your health.
달리기는 건강에 좋다.

2 Do you enjoy to walk in the forest?
너는 숲속에서 걷는 걸 좋아하니?

3 He hates waking up early.
그는 일찍 일어나는 것을 싫어한다.

4 I decided not going there.
나는 거기에 가지 않기로 결정했다.

5 I plan to go fishing.
나는 낚시하러 갈 계획이다.

6 Would you mind exchanging seats?
자리를 바꿀 수 있을까요?

7 I keep to make the same mistake over and over.
나는 같은 실수를 계속 반복해서 하고 있다.

8 We chose going by bus.
우리는 버스로 가기로 정했다.

9 I wish seeing you again.
다음에 또 볼 수 있으면 좋겠습니다.

10 She decided growing her hair.
그녀는 머리를 기르기로 결정했다.

11 I gave up try to help her.
나는 그녀를 돕는 것을 포기했다.

12 Exercising is good for your body.
운동하는 것은 몸에 좋다.

A 우리말과 같은 뜻이 되도록 보기 에서 알맞은 단어를 골라 쓰세요. (필요하면 형태를 바꾸세요.)

> 보기   go   jog   leave   play   read
> run   ski   stay   try   turn

1 He can keep ________________ for an hour.
그는 한 시간 동안 달리기를 할 수 있다.

2 Stop ________________ with your food!
음식 가지고 장난 그만 해!

3 Do you mind ________________ down the volume a little?
볼륨을 약간 줄여 줄래요?

4 I try to avoid ________________ shopping on Saturdays.
나는 토요일에 쇼핑하러 가는 것을 피하려고 한다.

5 I'm not planning ________________ here for long.
나는 오랫동안 여기에 머무를 계획이 없다.

6 He gave up ________________ a few years ago.
그는 몇 년 전에 조깅을 그만 두었다.

7 I was hoping ________________ here early today.
나는 오늘 일찍 여길 떠나길 바라고 있었다.

8 All my family enjoy ________________.
우리 가족은 모두 스키 타기를 즐긴다.

9 He keeps ________________ to win games.
그는 게임을 이기려고 계속 노력한다.

10 Did you finish ________________ that magazine?
너는 그 잡지를 다 읽었니?

B 주어진 동사를 알맞은 형태로 바꿔 빈칸에 쓰세요.

1 What do you want ________________? (eat)
너는 무엇을 먹고 싶니?

2 I go ________________ twice a week. (swim)
나는 일주일에 두 번 수영하러 간다.

3 They hope ________________ us next year. (visit)
그들은 내년에 우리를 방문하길 원한다.

4 The girl stopped ________________ and fell asleep. (cry)
그 소녀는 울기를 멈추고 잠들었다.

5 He can keep ________________ here. (work)
그는 여기서 계속 일할 수 있다.

6 Would you mind ________________ that again? (explain)
그거 다시 한 번 설명해 주시겠어요?

7 I finished ________________ the dishes. (do)
나는 설거지를 끝냈다.

8 I need ________________ some coffee. (drink)
나는 커피를 좀 마셔야겠다.

9 Katie chose ________________ by train. (go)
Katie는 기차를 타고 가기로 정했다.

10 I hate ________________ the dishes. (wash)
나는 설거지 하는 것을 싫어한다.

11 He avoids ________________ her. (meet)
그는 그녀를 만나기를 꺼린다.

12 They hope ________________ around two o'clock. (arrive)
그들은 2시경에 도착할 것으로 기대한다.

A 우리말과 같은 뜻이 되도록 주어진 말을 이용하여 문장을 완성하세요.

1 너는 이 책을 다 읽었니? (finish, read, this book)

→ Did you ______________________________________?

2 음악 소리 좀 낮춰 줄래요? (mind, turn down, the music)

→ Do you ______________________________________?

3 그는 몸무게를 1~2 파운드 줄일 필요가 있다. (need, lose)

→ He ______________________________________ a pound or two.

4 그녀는 2년 전에 가르치는 것을 그만두었다. (give up, teach)

→ She ______________________________________ two years ago.

5 그는 글쓰기를 멈추고 잠이 들었다. (stop, write)

→ He ______________________________________ and fell asleep.

6 나는 사람들을 만나고 새로운 곳을 보는 것을 즐긴다. (enjoy, meet, see)

→ I ____________________ people and ____________ new places.

7 그는 계속 내게 말을 걸려고 한다. (keep, try to, talk)

→ He ______________________________________ to me.

8 그는 Linda에 대해 말하기를 꺼린다. (avoid, talk)

→ He ______________________________________ about Linda.

9 제가 다음에 당신을 또 방문할 수 있으면 좋겠습니다. (wish, visit)

→ I ______________________________________ again.

10 나는 여기에 머무를 계획이다. (plan, stay)

→ I'm ______________________________________ here.

B 밑줄 친 부분을 바르게 고쳐 문장을 다시 쓰세요.

1 He hates <u>make</u> mistakes.   그는 실수하는 것을 싫어한다.

➡ ____

2 I don't mind <u>wait</u>.   나는 기다려도 괜찮다.

➡ ____

3 I need <u>going</u> to the bathroom.   나는 화장실에 가야 해.

➡ ____

4 Katie chose <u>staying</u> away from work that day.   Katie는 그날 일하지 않기로 했다.

➡ ____

5 He enjoys <u>to watch</u> birds.   그는 새 관찰을 즐긴다.

➡ ____

6 Stop <u>to talk</u> and listen!   이야기 그만하고 잘 들어라!

➡ ____

7 She needs <u>feeling</u> loved.   그녀는 사랑받는다고 느끼는 것이 필요하다.

➡ ____

8 I was <u>hoping to leaving</u> work early today.   나는 오늘 일찍 퇴근하길 바라고 있었다.

➡ ____

9 I hate <u>to leaving</u> home.   나는 집을 떠나기가 싫다.

➡ ____

10 He needs <u>losing</u> some weight.   그는 몸무게를 줄일 필요가 있다.

➡ ____

A 우리말과 같은 뜻이 되도록 주어진 말을 이용하여 문장을 완성하세요.

1 나는 혼자 있고 싶다. (want, be)

→ I ____________ ____________ ____________ alone.

2 나는 일주일에 한 번 수영하러 간다. (go, swim)

→ I ____________ ____________ once a week.

3 나는 설거지를 끝냈다. (finish, do the dishes)

→ I ____________ ____________ ____________ ____________.

4 Jones씨가 당신을 보기를 원한다. (wish, see)

→ Mr. Jones ____________ ____________ ____________ you.

5 그는 돌아오겠다고 약속했다. (promise, come)

→ He ____________ ____________ ____________ back.

6 자리를 바꿀 수 있을까요? (mind, exchange)

→ Would ____________ ____________ ____________ seats?

7 그들은 달리기 시작했다. (start, run)

→ They ____________ ____________ ____________.

8 그녀는 매일 걷는 것을 즐긴다. (enjoy, walk)

→ She ____________ ____________ daily.

9 나는 기차를 기다리는 게 싫다. (hate, wait for)

➡ I ______________ ______________ ______________ the train.

10 그녀는 머리를 기르기로 결정했다. (decide, grow)

➡ She ______________ ______________ ______________ her hair.

11 나는 낚시하러 갈 계획이다. (plan, go)

➡ I ______________ ______________ ______________ fishing.

12 나는 내 숙제하는 것을 끝냈다. (do my homework)

➡ ____

13 나는 일주일에 한 번 하이킹하러 간다. (hike)

➡ ____

14 나는 버스를 기다리는 게 싫다. (the bus)

➡ ____

15 창문을 열어도 될까요? (would, mind, open the window)

➡ ____

16 나는 농구 하는 것을 즐긴다. (play basketball)

➡ ____

17 그는 너를 만나기를 원한다. (wish, meet)

➡ ____

A 다음 단어를 두 번씩 듣고 따라 쓴 후 그 뜻을 쓰세요.

단어	두 번 따라 쓰기	뜻 쓰기
church 교회		
vacation 휴가		
wait 기다리다		
vase 꽃병		
pyramid 피라미드		
parents 부모		
barber 이발사		
clap 박수를 치다		
history 역사		
soldier 군인		
bench 벤치, 긴 의자		
rock 바위		
pass 지나다, 통과하다		

단어	두 번 따라 쓰기	뜻 쓰기
hill 언덕		
market 시장		
wallet 지갑		
pillow 베개		
science 과학		
gym 체육관		
bank 은행		
ant 개미		
flow 흐르다		
tower 탑		
temple 사원, 절		
potato 감자		
hunter 사냥꾼		

A 주어진 철자의 순서를 바르게 맞추어 우리말 뜻에 해당하는 단어를 쓰세요.

1 
lpca
박수를 치다

2 
ternuh
사냥꾼

3 
arkmet
시장

4 
hurcch
교회

5 
rewto
탑

6 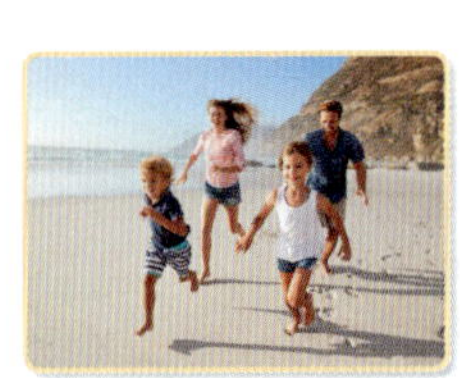
ticavaon
휴가

B 우리말과 같은 뜻이 되도록 보기 에서 알맞은 단어를 골라 쓰세요.

보기　　vase　　rock　　bank　　history　　hill

1 There is a gym in front of the ___________________.　은행 앞에 체육관이 있다.

2 They are coming down the ___________________.　그들은 언덕을 내려오고 있다.

3 A lion is sitting next to a ___________________.　사자가 바위 옆에 앉아 있다.

4 A ___________________ is on the table.　꽃병이 탁자 위에 있다.

5 She is reading a book about Korean ___________________.
그녀는 한국 역사에 관한 책을 읽고 있다.

C 다음 사진에 해당하는 단어를 아래 퍼즐에서 찾아 ○ 표시하고 빈칸에 쓰세요.

r	m	c	c	l	g	w	e	s	c
s	f	r	h	w	y	b	w	a	y
c	p	y	r	a	m	i	d	a	t
o	i	w	e	l	e	h	l	k	l
u	l	s	o	l	d	i	e	r	o
c	l	e	v	e	r	g	e	p	e
q	o	p	o	t	a	t	o	e	y
v	w	u	r	s	e	w	t	r	n

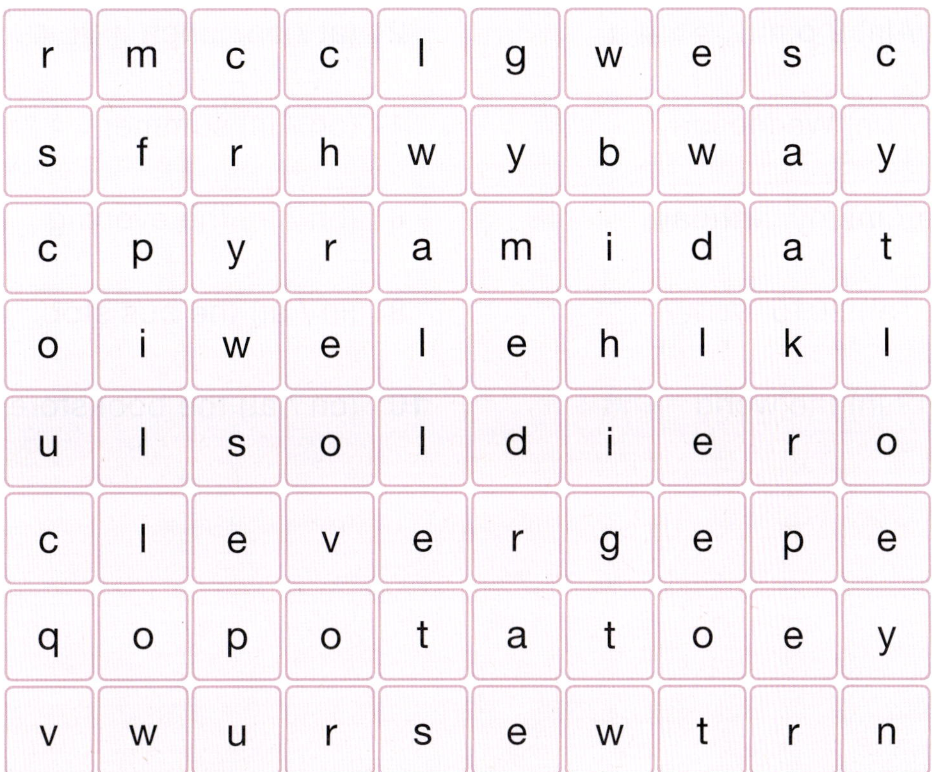

1. 체육관

2. 지갑

3. 피라미드

4. 감자

5. 군인

6. 베개

A ( ) 안에서 알맞은 전치사를 고르세요.

1 (at / in) 9 p.m. 오후 9시에

2 (at / on) lunch 점심 때

3 (at / on) Wednesday 수요일에

4 (on / in) summer 여름에

5 (on / in) my birthday 내 생일에

6 (on / in) the evening 저녁에

7 (in / at) 2015 2015년에

8 (in / at) the bus stop 버스 정류장에

9 (on / in) the world 세계에서

10 (on / at) the bookstore 서점에

B 우리말과 같은 뜻이 되도록 보기 에서 알맞은 말을 골라 쓰세요.

| 보기 | during | for | until | by |

1 He was in the hospital ________________ the winter.
그는 겨울 동안 병원에 입원해 있었다.

2 I will finish my homework ________________ nine.
나는 9시까지 숙제를 끝낼 것이다.

3 I waited for her ________________ five o'clock.
나는 그녀를 5시까지 기다렸다.

4 She went to Paris ________________ a week.
그녀는 일주일 동안 파리에 갔다.

C 밑줄 친 부분이 맞으면 ○, 틀리면 X 표시하세요.

1 Picasso was born <u>on</u> 1881.
피카소는 1881년에 태어났다.

2 I don't eat snacks <u>at</u> night.
나는 밤에 간식을 먹지 않는다.

3 Jenny and Fred live <u>in</u> Seoul.
Jenny와 Fred는 서울에 산다.

4 They stayed <u>at</u> the hotel.
그들은 그 호텔에 묵었다.

5 We will go shopping <u>in</u> the weekend.
우리는 주말에 쇼핑을 갈 것이다.

6 They were clapping <u>for</u> 10 minutes.
그들은 10분 동안 박수를 치고 있었다.

7 A baby is sleeping <u>at</u> her parents.
아기가 부모 사이에서 자고 있다.

8 There are soldiers <u>front to</u> the tent.
텐트 옆에 군인들이 있다.

9 I clean my bedroom <u>on</u> Saturday.
나는 토요일에 내 침실을 청소한다.

10 You should finish the work <u>until</u> Wednesday.
너는 수요일까지 그 일을 끝내야 한다.

11 Don't talk <u>for</u> the exam.
시험 중에는 말을 하지 마라.

12 There is a bottle <u>behind</u> the glass.
유리컵 뒤에 병이 하나 있다.

A 우리말과 같은 뜻이 되도록 빈칸에 알맞은 전치사를 쓰세요.

1 There is an umbrella _______________ the box.
상자 속에 우산이 있다.

2 A fly is sitting _______________ the wall.
벽 위에 파리가 한 마리 앉아 있다.

3 They stayed on the island _______________ the war.
그들은 전쟁 동안 그 섬에 머물렀다.

4 _______________ night, you can see the stars.
밤에는 별을 볼 수 있다.

5 She left her umbrella _______________ home.
그녀는 우산을 집에 두고 왔다.

6 She doesn't have any money _______________ her wallet.
그녀의 지갑 안에는 돈이 하나도 없다.

7 He watched TV _______________ the evening.
그는 저녁에 TV를 봤다.

8 There are many flowers here _______________ the spring.
여기는 봄에 많은 꽃들이 있다.

9 The barber slept _______________ lunchtime.
그 이발사는 점심시간 동안 잠을 잤다.

10 There is a small hill _______________ the house.
그 집 뒤에 작은 언덕이 있다.

11 The bus stops _______________ the market.
그 버스는 시장 앞에 선다.

12 Can I stay _______________ the weekend?
내가 주말까지 머물러도 되니?

B 우리말과 같은 뜻이 되도록 주어진 말을 이용하여 빈칸에 알맞은 말을 쓰세요.

1 그는 금요일에 수학 수업이 있다. (Friday)

➡ He has a math class ____________ ____________.

2 나는 9시까지 내 숙제를 끝낼 것이다. (nine)

➡ I will finish my homework ____________ ____________.

3 그 군인은 벤치에 앉았다. (the bench)

➡ The soldier sat ____________ ____________ ____________.

4 나는 매일 아침 6시에 일어난다. (6 o'clock)

➡ I get up ____________ ____________ ____________ every morning.

5 새장 안에는 새가 한 마리 있다. (the cage)

➡ There is a bird ____________ ____________ ____________.

6 그녀는 나무들 사이에 앉았다. (the trees)

➡ She sat ____________ ____________ ____________.

7 일주일 동안 비가 내렸다. (a week)

➡ It rained ____________ ____________ ____________.

8 나는 내 생일에 일찍 일어났다. (my birthday)

➡ I woke up early ____________ ____________ ____________.

A 우리말과 같은 뜻이 되도록 주어진 말을 이용하여 문장을 완성하세요.

1 A whale is swimming ________________________________. (the sea)
고래가 바다에서 헤엄치고 있다.

2 Can I stay ________________________________? (the weekend)
주말까지 있어도 될까요?

3 The bus stops ________________________________. (the hospital)
그 버스는 병원 앞에 정차한다.

4 It rains a lot on this island ________________________________. (the summer)
이 섬은 여름 동안 비가 많이 내린다.

5 My cat is sitting ________________________________. (the sofa)
내 고양이가 소파 뒤에 앉아 있다.

6 There is a black cat ________________________________. (the roof)
지붕 위에 검은 고양이가 있다.

7 There is a parking lot ________________________________. (the building)
그 건물 뒤에 주차장이 있다.

8 I will go camping ________________________________. (Saturday)
나는 토요일에 캠핑을 갈 것이다.

9 My younger brother was born ________________________________. (2017)
내 남동생은 2017년에 태어났다.

10 There is a market ________________________________. (the gym)
체육관 옆에 시장이 있다.

B 우리말과 같은 뜻이 되도록 밑줄 친 부분을 바르게 고쳐 문장을 다시 쓰세요.

1 My bike is <u>next to</u> the bookstore.　내 자전거는 서점 앞에 있다.

→ ____

2 A river flows <u>in</u> the two mountains.　두 산 사이로 강이 흐른다.

→ ____

3 I visited my grandmother <u>at</u> New Year's Day.　나는 설날에 할머니를 찾아뵈었다.

→ ____

4 I will finish the homework <u>until</u> Thursday.　그 숙제를 목요일까지 마칠게요.

→ ____

5 The post office is <u>behind</u> the library.　우체국은 도서관 옆에 있다.

→ ____

6 It rained a lot <u>by</u> the morning.　아침 동안 비가 많이 내렸다.

→ ____

7 They arrived late <u>on</u> the airport.　그들은 공항에 늦게 도착했다.

→ ____

8 The museum closes <u>in</u> 5 p.m.　그 박물관은 오후 5시에 문을 닫는다.

→ ____

9 A bird is sitting <u>over</u> your hat.　네 모자 위에 새가 앉아 있어.

→ ____

10 I'm going to study math <u>by</u> 5 p.m.　나는 오후 5시까지 수학을 공부할 거야.

→ ____

A 우리말과 같은 뜻이 되도록 주어진 말을 이용하여 문장을 완성하세요.

1 그녀는 생일에 많은 선물을 받았다. (her birthday)

→ She got a lot of gifts ＿＿＿＿＿＿ ＿＿＿＿＿＿ ＿＿＿＿＿＿.

2 그는 휴식하는 동안 만화책을 읽었다. (the break)

→ He read comic books ＿＿＿＿＿＿ ＿＿＿＿＿＿ ＿＿＿＿＿＿.

3 배낭이 책상 아래 있다. (the desk)

→ The backpack is ＿＿＿＿＿＿ ＿＿＿＿＿＿ ＿＿＿＿＿＿.

4 나는 오후에 슈퍼마켓에 갔다. (the afternoon)

→ I went to the supermarket ＿＿＿＿＿＿ ＿＿＿＿＿＿ ＿＿＿＿＿＿.

5 아이들이 버스 정류장에서 스쿨버스를 기다린다. (the bus stop)

→ Children wait for the school bus ＿＿＿＿＿＿ ＿＿＿＿＿＿

＿＿＿＿＿＿ ＿＿＿＿＿＿.

6 그들은 아침 식사 때 차를 마신다. (breakfast)

→ They drink tea ＿＿＿＿＿＿ ＿＿＿＿＿＿.

7 모니터 뒤에 모기가 한 마리 있다. (the monitor)

→ There is a mosquito ＿＿＿＿＿＿ ＿＿＿＿＿＿ ＿＿＿＿＿＿.

8 사자가 바위 옆에 앉아 있다. (rock)

→ A lion is sitting ＿＿＿＿＿＿ ＿＿＿＿＿＿ a ＿＿＿＿＿＿.

9 두 섬 사이로 배가 한 척이 지나간다. (islands)

→ A ship passes _____________ the _____________ _____________.

10 개 한 마리가 탁자 아래 누워 있다. (the table)

→ A dog is lying _____________ _____________ _____________.

11 그들은 여름에 바다에 간다. (the summer)

→ They go to the sea _____________ _____________ _____________.

12 그들은 밤에 우유를 마신다. (milk, night)

→ ____

13 배낭이 의자 위에 있다. (the chair)

→ ____

14 그는 낮 동안에 잡지를 읽었다. (magazines, the day)

→ ____

15 사자가 바위 앞에 앉아 있다. (in front of, a rock)

→ ____

16 그들은 겨울에 산에 간다. (the mountains, winter)

→ ____

17 모니터 뒤에 파리가 한 마리 있다. (a fly)

→ ____

A 다음 단어를 두 번씩 듣고 따라 쓴 후 그 뜻을 쓰세요.

단어	두 번 따라 쓰기	뜻 쓰기
ladder 사다리		
stair 계단		
village 마을		
eagle 독수리		
fly 날다, 파리		
diving 다이빙		
tunnel 터널		
square 광장		
hole 구멍		
glasses 안경		
blond 금발의		
starfish 불가사리		
balloon 풍선		

단어	두 번 따라 쓰기		뜻 쓰기
frog 개구리			
stream 개울			
bakery 제과점			
desert 사막			
cloud 구름			
pear 배			
sweet 달콤한			
bubble 거품			
princess 공주			
pumpkin 호박			
roof 지붕			
mosquito 모기			
butterfly 나비			

A 주어진 철자의 순서를 바르게 맞추어 우리말 뜻에 해당하는 단어를 쓰세요.

1 
rtsede
사막

2
nelnut
터널

3
assgles
안경

4
pkpumin
호박

5 
flytterbu
나비

6
moquisot
모기

B 우리말과 같은 뜻이 되도록 보기 에서 알맞은 단어를 골라 쓰세요.

보기   stairs   village   flying   hole   bubbles

1 An eagle is _______________ high up in the sky.   독수리가 하늘 위로 높이 날고 있다.

2 She is coming down the _______________.   그녀가 계단 아래로 내려오고 있다.

3 A fly came in through the _______________.   파리가 구멍을 통해 들어왔다.

4 The _______________ start to go up.   거품이 위로 올라가기 시작한다.

5 She drove through the _______________.   그녀는 마을을 통과해서 차를 몰았다.

C 다음 사진에 해당하는 단어를 아래 퍼즐에서 찾아 ○ 표시하고 빈칸에 쓰세요.

c	b	q	a	c	h	g	w	e	s
y	s	e	b	a	k	e	r	y	a
t	c	l	a	d	d	e	r	e	a
p	e	g	l	r	o	c	o	t	k
e	a	g	l	e	u	d	o	l	e
a	r	l	o	e	x	q	f	d	h
r	t	r	o	n	g	e	n	a	e
n	h	n	n	r	s	n	w	t	r

1

제과점

2

사다리

3

독수리

4

배

5

지붕

6

풍선

A 우리말과 같은 뜻이 되도록 (   ) 안에서 알맞은 것을 고르세요.

1 We are going (to / from) the post office.   우리는 우체국에 가는 중이다.

2 The light came (down / through) the window.   불빛이 창문을 통해 들어왔다.

3 She studied (about / with) monkeys.   그녀는 원숭이에 관해 연구했다.

4 He is walking in the desert (like / without) a hat.   그는 모자 없이 사막을 걷고 있다.

5 She went to London (by / with) airplane.   그녀는 비행기를 타고 런던에 갔다.

6 She came (across / through) the street to see me.   그녀가 도로를 가로질러 나를 보러 왔다.

7 Why does an apple fall (down / through)?   사과는 왜 아래로 떨어질까?

8 The basketball player is (about / like) two meters tall.   그 농구 선수는 키가 대략 2미터이다.

B 우리말과 같은 뜻이 되도록 보기 에서 알맞은 단어를 골라 쓰세요.

보기	with	without	up	down

1 The plane is flying _______________ in the sky.
비행기가 하늘을 날고 있다.

2 I saw a girl _______________ red hair yesterday.
나는 어제 빨간 머리를 한 소녀를 보았다.

3 A bear was running _______________ the hill.
곰 한 마리가 언덕을 달려 내려오고 있었다.

4 Don't go shopping _______________ me.
나 없이 쇼핑하러 가지 마.

C 밑줄 친 부분이 우리말과 같은 뜻이면 ○, 다르면 X 표시하세요.

1 We can't live <u>without</u> love.
우리는 사랑 없이는 살 수 없어.

2 She wrote a book <u>about</u> flowers.
그녀는 꽃에 관한 책을 썼다.

3 Sunlight comes in <u>across</u> the hole.
구멍을 통해 햇빛이 들어온다.

4 My brother is very tall <u>by</u> you.
내 오빠는 너처럼 키가 매우 크다.

5 You can't see the movie <u>without</u> tears.
그 영화는 눈물 없이는 볼 수 없다.

6 The man ate lunch <u>with</u> his sister.
그 남자는 그의 여동생과 점심을 먹었다.

7 A lot of snow fell <u>through</u> the sky.
많은 눈이 하늘에서 내렸다.

8 He slowly went <u>up</u> the hill.
그는 천천히 언덕을 내려갔다.

9 I want to go fishing <u>with</u> you.
나는 너와 함께 낚시하러 가고 싶다.

10 A horse ran <u>through</u> the field.
말 한 마리가 들판을 가로질러 달렸다.

11 The rocks are falling <u>up</u>.
바위들이 아래로 떨어지고 있다.

12 She runs very fast <u>like</u> a deer.
그녀는 사슴처럼 매우 빨리 달린다.

A 우리말과 같은 뜻이 되도록 보기 에서 알맞은 단어를 골라 쓰세요.

> 보기　　across　　by　　down　　like　　through
> 　　　　　to　　up　　with　　without

1 The pear was very sweet ________________ honey.
그 배는 꿀처럼 매우 달았다.

2 I want to go to the moon ________________ rocket.
나는 로켓을 타고 달에 가고 싶다.

3 Look at that child ________________ big eyes.
커다란 눈을 가진 저 아이를 봐.

4 We can't live ________________ air.
우리는 공기 없이는 살 수 없다.

5 The man ran away ________________ the window.
그 남자는 창문을 통해 도망쳤다.

6 The bird climbed ________________ to the clouds.
그 새는 구름 위로 올라갔다.

7 The boy often goes ________________ the bakery.
그 남자아이는 빵집에 자주 간다.

8 A cat is walking ________________ the grass.
고양이 한 마리가 풀밭을 가로질러 걸어가고 있다.

9 The boy is coming ________________ the stairs.
그 남자아이가 계단 아래로 내려오고 있다.

B 우리말과 같은 뜻이 되도록 주어진 말을 이용하여 빈칸에 알맞은 말을 쓰세요.

1 그녀는 그녀의 가족과 함께 저녁을 먹었다. (her family)

→ She had dinner ＿＿＿＿＿＿ ＿＿＿＿＿＿ ＿＿＿＿＿＿.

2 그는 자전거를 타고 학교에 간다. (bicycle)

→ He goes to school ＿＿＿＿＿＿ ＿＿＿＿＿＿.

3 그녀는 마을을 통과해서 차를 몰았다. (the village)

→ She drove ＿＿＿＿＿＿ ＿＿＿＿＿＿ ＿＿＿＿＿＿.

4 그녀는 도로를 가로질러 뛰었다. (the road)

→ She ran ＿＿＿＿＿＿ ＿＿＿＿＿＿ ＿＿＿＿＿＿.

5 그녀는 한국 역사에 관한 책을 읽고 있다. (Korean history)

→ She is reading a book ＿＿＿＿＿＿ ＿＿＿＿＿＿ ＿＿＿＿＿＿.

6 내 남동생은 걸어서 학교에 간다. (foot)

→ My brother goes to school ＿＿＿＿＿＿ ＿＿＿＿＿＿.

7 그녀는 마스크 없이 외출했다. (a mask)

→ She went out ＿＿＿＿＿＿ ＿＿＿＿＿＿ ＿＿＿＿＿＿.

8 그는 말처럼 매우 빨리 달린다. (horse)

→ He runs very fast ＿＿＿＿＿＿ ＿＿＿＿＿＿ ＿＿＿＿＿＿.

A 우리말과 같은 뜻이 되도록 주어진 말을 이용하여 문장을 완성하세요.

1 The leaf is ________________________________. (fall)
나뭇잎이 아래로 떨어지고 있다.

2 She ran ________________________________. (the playground)
그녀는 운동장을 가로질러 달렸다.

3 This candy tastes ________________________________. (an orange)
이 캔디는 오렌지 같은 맛이 난다.

4 She wrote an essay ________________________________. (a cat)
그녀는 고양이에 관한 수필을 썼다.

5 A mosquito came in ________________________________. (the hole)
모기 한 마리가 구멍을 통해 들어왔다.

6 An apple fell ________________________________. (the tree)
사과 하나가 나무에서 떨어졌다.

7 A motorcycle is going ________________________________. (the hill)
오토바이가 언덕을 올라가고 있다.

8 My uncle went to the island ________________________________. (ship)
내 삼촌은 배를 타고 그 섬에 갔다.

9 He played soccer ________________________________. (friends)
그는 그의 친구들과 축구를 했다.

10 The fruit looks ________________________________. (a pumpkin)
그 과일은 호박처럼 생겼다.

B 우리말과 같은 뜻이 되도록 밑줄 친 부분을 바르게 고쳐 문장을 다시 쓰세요.

1 Don't go camping <u>with</u> me.　나 없이 캠핑하러 가지 마.

→ ____

2 A bee came in <u>across</u> the window.　벌 한 마리가 창문으로 들어왔다.

→ ____

3 Butterflies fly from flower <u>of</u> flower.　나비들이 꽃에서 꽃으로 날아다닌다.

→ ____

4 A starfish looks <u>about</u> a star.　불가사리는 별처럼 생겼다.

→ ____

5 Look at the girl <u>by</u> blond hair.　금발머리를 가진 소녀를 보세요.

→ ____

6 An iguana is climbing <u>on</u> the wall.　이구아나가 벽을 올라가고 있다.

→ ____

7 My family will go <u>from</u> the zoo.　우리 가족은 동물원에 갈 것이다.

→ ____

8 He ran <u>down</u> the square.　그는 광장을 가로질러 달렸다.

→ ____

9 A balloon is coming <u>up</u> to the ground.　풍선이 땅으로 내려오고 있다.

→ ____

10 The baby smiles <u>through</u> an angel.　그 아기는 천사처럼 웃는다.

→ ____

A 우리말과 같은 뜻이 되도록 주어진 말을 이용하여 문장을 완성하세요.

1 나는 택시를 타고 집에 가고 싶다. (taxi)

→ I want to go home ____________ ____________.

2 그는 대략 두 시간 동안 잤다. (hours)

→ He slept for ____________ ____________ ____________.

3 그 바위는 코끼리처럼 생겼다. (an elephant)

→ The rock looks ____________ ____________ ____________.

4 그는 그의 부모님 없이 동물원에 갔다. (his parents)

→ He went to the zoo ____________ ____________ ____________.

5 그 기차는 숲을 통과하고 있다. (the forest)

→ The train is passing ____________ ____________ ____________.

6 그는 다이빙대에서 뛰어내렸다. (diving board)

→ He jumped down ____________ the ____________ ____________.

7 많은 새들이 땅으로 내려오고 있다. (the ground)

→ Many birds are coming down ____________ ____________ ____________.

8 한 아이가 방을 가로질러 걸어가고 있다. (the room)

→ A child is walking ____________ ____________ ____________.

9 나는 동물들에 관한 책을 읽고 있다. (animals)

→ I'm reading a book ______________ ____________.

10 그녀는 우체국으로 달려갔다. (the post office)

→ She ran ____________ ______________ __________ ____________.

11 긴 꼬리를 가진 생쥐를 봐라. (the long tail)

→ Look at the mouse __________ __________ _________ _________.

12 그는 그의 부모님 없이 병원에 갔다. (the hospital)

→ ____

13 그 바위는 사자처럼 생겼다. (a lion)

→ ____

14 그는 대략 한 시간 동안 잤다. (an hour)

→ ____

15 한 아이가 도로를 가로질러 걸어가고 있다. (the street)

→ ____

16 나는 버스를 타고 집에 가고 싶다. (want, bus)

→ ____

17 나는 고양이와 개에 관한 책을 읽었다. (cats and dogs)

→ ____

A 다음 단어를 두 번씩 듣고 따라 쓴 후 그 뜻을 쓰세요.

단어	두 번 따라 쓰기	뜻 쓰기
neighbor 이웃		
cinema 영화관		
clear 치우다		
company 회사		
post 게시하다, 올리다		
website 웹사이트		
weep 울다		
bark 짖다		
loudly 큰 소리로		
tasty 맛있는		
windy 바람이 많이 부는		
medicine 약		
bitter 맛이 쓴		

단어	두 번 따라 쓰기	뜻 쓰기
order 주문하다		
bowl 그릇		
add 첨가하다		
slice 조각, 부분		
lonely 외로운		
borrow 빌리다		
silent 조용한		
perfect 완벽한		
culture 문화		
successful 성공한		
equipment 장비		
airport 공항		
discussion 토의, 논의		

A 주어진 철자의 순서를 바르게 맞추어 우리말 뜻에 해당하는 단어를 쓰세요.

1 
arbk
짖다

2 
icmena
영화관

3 
oludyl
큰 소리로

4 
panycom
회사

5 
sitebew
웹사이트

6 
lyloen
외로운

B 우리말과 같은 뜻이 되도록 보기 에서 알맞은 단어를 골라 쓰세요. (필요하면 형태를 바꾸세요.)

보기   add   borrow   clear   culture   post

1 _________________ a few slices of oranges.   오렌지 몇 조각을 추가해라.

2 They study American _________________.   그들은 미국 문화를 공부한다.

3 I _________________ a new book from the library.   나는 도서관에서 새 책을 빌렸다.

4 The man _________________ the snow from outside his home.
그 남자는 집 밖의 눈을 치웠다.

5 He _________________ a message on Twitter.   그는 트위터에 메시지를 올렸다.

C 다음 사진에 해당하는 단어를 아래 퍼즐에서 찾아 ○ 표시하고 빈칸에 쓰세요.

c	n	n	i	t	x	o	c	s	s
y	o	s	i	l	e	n	t	w	a
t	w	l	e	p	t	a	c	c	e
n	e	i	g	h	b	o	r	i	k
o	l	c	c	s	o	r	d	e	r
v	m	e	d	i	w	i	n	d	y
q	i	u	a	a	l	o	l	m	e
n	b	a	r	t	s	e	a	a	r

1 

이웃

2 

조용한

3 

주문하다

4 

조각, 부분

5 

바람이 많이 부는

6 

그릇

A 밑줄 친 부분이 맞으면 ◯, 틀리면 X 표시하세요.

1 You look <u>sleepy</u>.
너는 졸려 보인다.

2 That dress looks <u>beautifully</u>.
저 드레스는 아름다워 보인다.

3 The ice cream was <u>taste</u>.
아이스크림은 맛있었다.

4 It was <u>windy</u> last night.
어젯밤에는 바람이 많이 불었다.

5 A good medicine tastes <u>bitter</u>.
좋은 약은 입에 쓰다.

6 They feel <u>happily</u>.
그들은 행복하다고 느낀다.

7 Mom loves <u>I</u> and my brother.
엄마는 나와 내 남동생을 사랑하신다.

8 The sky turned <u>dark</u> after lunch.
하늘이 점심 이후에 어둡게 변했다.

9 The young singer became <u>famously</u>.
그 젊은 가수는 유명해졌다.

10 The weather today looks <u>cold</u>.
오늘 날씨는 추워 보인다.

B 다음 중 맞는 문장을 고르세요.

1 모든 사람은 때로 슬프다고 느낀다.
ⓐ Everyone feels sad at times.
ⓑ Everyone feels sadly at times.

2 그녀는 회의를 하는 동안 잠자코 있었다.
ⓐ She kept silent during the meeting.
ⓑ She kept silently during the meeting.

3 그 스테이크는 맛있는 냄새가 난다.
ⓐ The steak smells deliciously.
ⓑ The steak smells delicious.

4 8시에 극장 밖에서 그를 만날 거야.
ⓐ I'll meet he outside the theater at 8:00.
ⓑ I'll meet him outside the theater at 8:00.

5 나는 그녀가 정말 그리울 거야.
ⓐ I will miss her so much.
ⓑ I will miss she so much.

6 그녀는 아주 완벽해 보인다.
ⓐ She looks so perfect.
ⓑ She looks so perfectly.

7 내 여동생은 울었다.
ⓐ My little sister wept.
ⓑ My little sister weeping.

A (　) 안에서 알맞은 것을 고르세요.

1 He seems (nice / nicely).
그는 멋져 보인다.

2 Dinner smells (good / deliciously).
저녁 식사가 맛있는 냄새가 난다.

3 The pie tastes (greatly / great).
파이가 맛이 아주 좋다.

4 We (baked / baked to) some cookies.
우리는 과자를 좀 구웠다.

5 She was (eating / eating for) a sandwich.
그녀는 샌드위치를 먹고 있었다.

6 She (likes / likes to) comic books very much.
그녀는 만화책을 무척 좋아한다.

7 The company (makes / makes for) computers.
그 회사는 컴퓨터를 만든다.

8 He (posted to / posted) a message on a website.
그는 웹사이트에 메시지를 올렸다.

9 I (bought / bought for) a new cap yesterday.
나는 어제 새 모자를 샀다.

10 She (wants / wants to) a new phone.
그녀는 새로운 전화기를 갖고 싶어 한다.

11 I (changed with / changed) trains to get there.
나는 거기에 가려고 기차를 갈아탔다.

12 I didn't (eat / eat for) any meat.
나는 고기를 전혀 먹지 않았다.

B 밑줄 친 부분을 바르게 고쳐 쓰세요.

1 Cathy <u>tall</u>.
Cathy는 키가 크다.

→ ___________________

2 She <u>became to</u> a doctor.
그녀는 의사가 되었다.

→ ___________________

3 He <u>working</u>.
그는 일하고 있다.

→ ___________________

4 My dad likes <u>to steak</u>.
우리 아빠는 스테이크를 좋아하신다.

→ ___________________

5 The bell <u>is rang</u>.
벨이 울렸다.

→ ___________________

6 Jack is <u>busily</u> these days.
Jack은 요즘 바쁘다.

→ ___________________

7 The bus came <u>lately</u>.
버스가 늦게 왔다.

→ ___________________

8 I <u>ordered to</u> a pizza for lunch.
나는 점심으로 피자를 주문했다.

→ ___________________

9 Do you <u>ride to</u> your bike on Sundays?
너는 일요일마다 자전거를 타니?

→ ___________________

10 My brother helps <u>I</u> a lot.
우리 형은 나를 많이 도와준다.

→ ___________________

11 <u>Add to</u> two slices of ham.
두 장의 햄을 더 얹어라.

→ ___________________

12 I really <u>miss for</u> my friends.
나는 내 친구들이 정말 그립다.

→ ___________________

A 우리말과 같은 뜻이 되도록 보기 에서 알맞은 단어를 골라 쓰세요.

보기	bad	better	bitter	cute	good
	great	late	lonely	well	interesting

1 These dancers jump ________________.
이 무용수들은 점프를 잘한다.

2 The book becomes ________________ in Chapter 2.
그 책은 두 번째 챕터부터 흥미로워진다.

3 Do you sometimes feel ________________?
너는 가끔 외롭다고 느끼니?

4 Yeah, that sounds ________________!
응, 정말 좋은 생각이야!

5 The puppy looks ________________.
그 강아지는 귀여워 보인다.

6 Mm! This tastes ________________!
음! 이건 맛이 좋은데!

7 The food tasted ________________ than it looked.
그 음식은 보기보다 맛이 좋았다.

8 That dress looks pretty ________________.
저 드레스는 상당히 안 좋아 보인다.

9 The train is a half hour ________________.
그 기차는 30분 늦었다.

10 This medicine tastes ________________.
이 약은 맛이 쓰다.

B 밑줄 친 부분을 바르게 고쳐 문장을 다시 쓰세요.

1 She was <u>sickness</u>.   그녀는 아팠다.

→ ____

2 He <u>a bicycle wants</u> for his birthday.   그는 생일 선물로 자전거를 원한다.

→ ____

3 You look <u>happiness</u> today.   너는 오늘 행복해 보이는구나.

→ ____

4 That person gets <u>angrily</u> very easily.   저 사람은 매우 쉽게 화를 낸다.

→ ____

5 We all want to become <u>richly</u>, right?   우리 모두는 부자가 되길 원해, 그렇지?

→ ____

6 Why do we <u>love to</u> music?   우리는 왜 음악을 사랑할까?

→ ____

7 I <u>wearing</u> glasses for reading.   나는 책을 읽을 때 안경을 쓴다.

→ ____

8 She hit him <u>hardly</u>.   그녀는 그를 세게 때렸다.

→ ____

9 I <u>bought for</u> a new dress yesterday.   나는 어제 새 드레스를 샀다.

→ ____

10 I <u>borrowed for</u> his book yesterday.   나는 어제 그의 책을 빌렸다.

→ ____

A 우리말과 같은 뜻이 되도록 주어진 말을 이용하여 문장을 완성하세요.

1 나는 그의 펜을 빌렸다. (borrow, his pen)

→ I ＿＿＿＿＿＿ ＿＿＿＿＿＿ ＿＿＿＿＿＿.

2 그들은 그것을 하지 않았다. (do, that)

→ They ＿＿＿＿＿＿ ＿＿＿＿＿＿ ＿＿＿＿＿＿.

3 음식은 맛있고 신선했다. (tasty, fresh)

→ The food was ＿＿＿＿＿＿ ＿＿＿＿＿＿ ＿＿＿＿＿＿.

4 그들은 그것을 하지 않았다. (do, that)

→ They ＿＿＿＿＿＿ ＿＿＿＿＿＿ ＿＿＿＿＿＿.

5 그녀는 시험에 합격하기 위해 열심히 공부했다. (study, hard)

→ ＿＿＿＿＿＿ ＿＿＿＿＿＿ ＿＿＿＿＿＿ to pass the exam.

6 너는 지금 기분이 나아졌니? (better, feel)

→ Do ＿＿＿＿＿＿ ＿＿＿＿＿＿ ＿＿＿＿＿＿ now?

7 하늘이 점심 이후에 빨갛게 변했다. (red, turn)

→ The sky ＿＿＿＿＿＿ ＿＿＿＿＿＿ after lunch.

8 너는 이 색깔을 좋아하니? (this color, like)

→ Do you ＿＿＿＿＿＿ ＿＿＿＿＿＿ ＿＿＿＿＿＿?

9 그 소녀는 시간이 더 필요하니? (more time, need)

→ Does the girl _____________ _____________ _____________?

10 나는 시험에서 실수를 했다. (make, a mistake)

→ I _____________ _____________ _____________ on the test.

11 어제는 더웠다. (it, hot)

→ _____________ _____________ _____________ yesterday.

12 나는 그의 책을 빌렸다. (borrow, book)

→ ____

13 음식은 차갑고 건조했다. (cold, dry)

→ ____

14 너는 이 영화를 좋아하니? (this movie, like)

→ ____

15 너는 시간이 더 필요하니? (need)

→ ____

16 그는 기차를 갈아탔다. (trains, change)

→ ____

17 어제는 추웠다. (cold)

→ ____

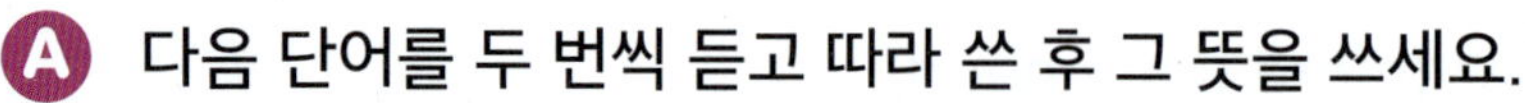

A 다음 단어를 두 번씩 듣고 따라 쓴 후 그 뜻을 쓰세요.

단어	두 번 따라 쓰기	뜻 쓰기
send 보내다		
lend 빌려주다		
elect 선출하다		
president 대통령		
liar 거짓말쟁이		
garlic 마늘		
awful 끔찍한		
thirsty 목이 마른		
secret 비밀		
wet 젖은		
attractive 매력적인		
fear 두려움, 공포		
judge 판사, 심판		

단어	두 번 따라 쓰기	뜻 쓰기
guilty 유죄의		
prove 증명하다		
laptop 노트북 컴퓨터		
favorite 가장 좋아하는		
purple 자주색		
chairman 의장		
pay 지불하다		
offer 제안하다		
upset 속상한		
spinach 시금치		
useful 쓸모 있는		
truth 진실		
nail 손톱		

A 주어진 철자의 순서를 바르게 맞추어 우리말 뜻에 해당하는 단어를 쓰세요.

1  eldn
빌려주다

2  gacirl
마늘

3  oerff
제안하다

4  spachni
시금치

5  anli
손톱

6  manchiar
의장

B 우리말과 같은 뜻이 되도록 보기 에서 알맞은 단어를 골라 쓰세요.

| 보기 | attractive   awful   send   favorite   thirsty |

1 Will you ______________ her a letter?   너는 그녀에게 편지를 보낼 거니?

2 I don't really find her ______________.   나는 그녀가 그렇게 매력적인지는 모르겠다.

3 The salty food made her ______________.   짠 음식이 그녀를 목마르게 했다.

4 It will make the soup ______________.   그것이 수프를 아주 맛없게 만들 것이다.

5 I'll show you my ______________ clothes.   내가 가장 좋아하는 옷들을 너에게 보여줄게.

C 다음 사진에 해당하는 단어를 아래 퍼즐에서 찾아 ○ 표시하고 빈칸에 쓰세요.

r	s	r	c	l	g	w	e	s	c
s	p	u	r	p	l	e	l	l	y
c	n	s	k	p	i	l	e	a	t
g	a	e	l	i	f	e	a	r	l
u	i	f	u	n	s	c	t	e	o
c	l	u	p	s	e	t	e	p	e
q	b	l	a	p	t	o	p	e	y
v	n	u	r	h	e	w	t	r	n

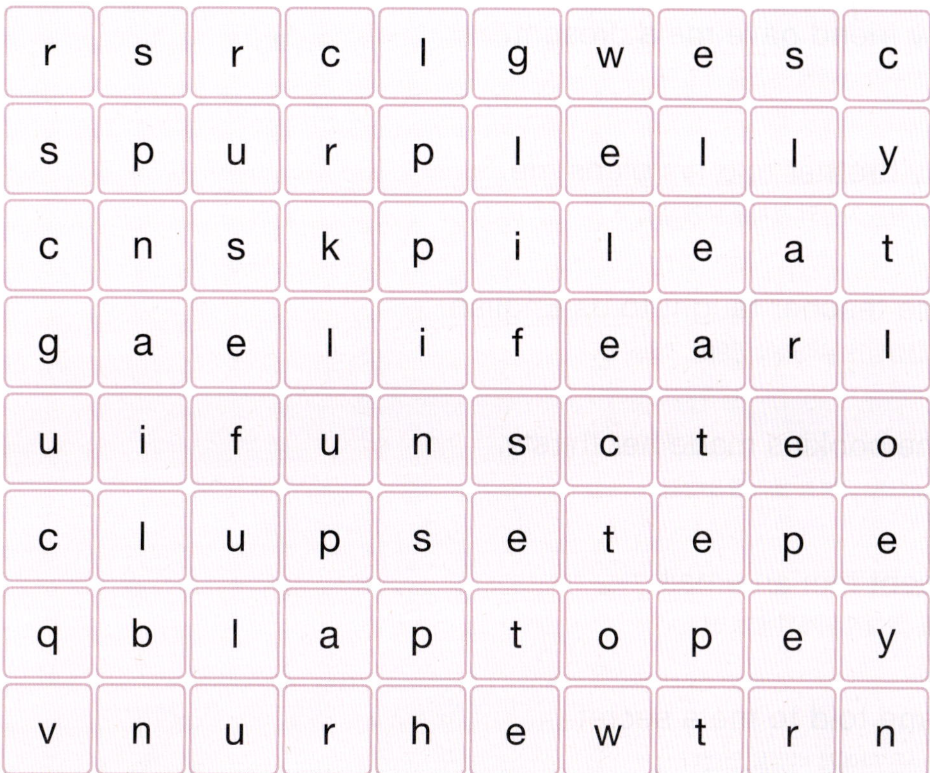

1
자주색

2
노트북 컴퓨터

3
속상한

4
선출하다

5
쓸모 있는

6
두려움, 공포

A 밑줄 친 부분이 맞으면 ○, 틀리면 X 표시하세요.

1 My friend gave me a present.
내 친구가 나에게 선물을 주었다.

2 My brother told his plans me.
우리 형은 자신의 계획을 내게 말했다.

3 The teacher taught to us English.
그 선생님은 우리에게 영어를 가르치셨다.

4 The cookies made her thirsty.
그 과자는 그녀를 목마르게 했다.

5 I sent him an email.
나는 그에게 이메일을 보냈다.

6 Jane told to me a secret.
Jane은 나에게 비밀을 말했다.

7 He bought for me a cap.
그는 나에게 모자를 사 주었다.

8 The rain made all of us wet.
비가 우리 모두를 젖게 했다.

9 Homework often makes tired me.
숙제는 종종 나를 지치게 한다.

10 She found the work boring.
그녀는 그 일이 따분하다고 느꼈다.

B 다음 중 맞는 문장을 고르세요.

1 Cathy가 네게 케이크를 만들어 줄 것이다.

ⓐ Cathy will make you a cake.

ⓑ Cathy will make a cake you.

2 그들은 그를 미국의 대통령으로 선출했다.

ⓐ They elected him president of the U.S.

ⓑ They elected him to president of the U.S.

3 나를 거짓말쟁이라고 부르지 마.

ⓐ Don't call I a liar.

ⓑ Don't call me a liar.

4 너는 나를 행복하게 해.

ⓐ You make happy me.

ⓑ You make me happy.

5 나는 그 영화가 아주 훌륭하다는 것을 알게 되었다.

ⓐ I found the movie wonderful.

ⓑ I found wonderful the movie.

6 내 머리를 짧게 잘라 줘.

ⓐ Cut my hair short.

ⓑ Cut short my hair.

7 엄마는 내 여동생에게 스웨터를 만들어주셨다.

ⓐ Mom made my sister a sweater.

ⓑ Mom made to my sister a sweater.

A (　) 안에서 알맞은 것을 고르세요.

1　Harry (sent / sent to) her some flowers.
Harry는 그녀에게 꽃을 좀 보냈다.

2　I'll (show / show to) you my favorite photos.
내가 가장 좋아하는 사진들을 너에게 보여줄게.

3　Chocolate makes Mary (happiness / happy).
초콜릿은 Mary를 행복하게 한다.

4　They elected (Mike chairman / chairman Mike).
그들은 Mike를 의장으로 선출했다.

5　Can you pay (she / her) the money?
당신은 그녀에게 그 돈을 지불할 수 있나요?

6　He made Neil (to upset / upset).
그는 Neil을 화나게 했다.

7　Public speaking makes Henry (nervous / nervously).
대중들 앞에서 말하는 것은 Henry를 불안하게 한다.

8　Can I ask (to you / you) something?
너에게 뭐 좀 물어봐도 되니?

9　She taught (science us / us science).
그녀는 우리에게 과학을 가르치셨다.

10　She gave (I / me) an English book.
그녀는 내게 영어책을 주었다.

11　The box keeps vegetables (fresh / freshly) for longer.
그 상자는 야채를 더 오랫동안 신선하게 보관한다.

12　A lot of women find him (attractive / attract).
많은 여성들은 그를 매력적이라고 생각한다.

B 우리말과 같은 뜻이 되도록 주어진 말을 바르게 배열하세요.

1 Mary showed (her / him / pictures). ➔ ________________________
Mary는 그에게 자신의 사진들을 보여주었다.

2 Jim sent (friend / a gift / his). ➔ ________________________
Jim은 그의 친구에게 선물을 보냈다.

3 The news (made / sad / her). ➔ ________________________
그 소식은 그녀를 슬프게 했다.

4 Fear (them / kept / quiet). ➔ ________________________
공포가 그들을 조용하게 했다.

5 She called (a liar / her / friend). ➔ ________________________
그녀는 자기 친구를 거짓말쟁이라고 불렀다.

6 He (the work / found / interesting). ➔ ________________________
그는 그 일이 흥미롭다고 생각했다.

7 Time (proved / wrong / them). ➔ ________________________
시간이 지나서 그들이 틀렸다는 것이 밝혀졌다.

8 I will (you / tell / the story). ➔ ________________________
내가 너에게 이야기를 해줄게.

9 You (me / crazy / drive). ➔ ________________________
너는 나를 미치게 하는구나.

10 My brother (taught / English / me). ➔ ________________________
내 형은 나에게 영어를 가르쳐주었다.

11 He painted (purple / box / the). ➔ ________________________
그는 그 상자를 보라색으로 칠했다.

12 They named (their / John / son). ➔ ________________________
그들은 그들의 아들 이름을 John이라고 지었다.

A 우리말과 같은 뜻이 되도록 보기에서 알맞은 단어를 골라 쓰세요. (필요하면 형태를 바꾸세요.)

> 보기   buy   call   elect   find   keep
>   make   send   show   paint   tell

1 My dad ________________ me a bike.
아빠는 내게 자전거를 사 주셨다.

2 Mom ________________ me a pretty doll.
엄마는 내게 예쁜 인형을 만들어주셨다.

3 Mike ________________ Sally his new laptop.
Mike는 Sally에게 그의 새 노트북 컴퓨터를 보여주었다.

4 I want to ________________ my walls blue.
나는 내 벽을 파란색으로 칠하고 싶다.

5 I will ________________ the hotel an email to check the prices.
나는 가격을 확인하기 위해 호텔에 메일을 보낼 것이다.

6 Please ________________ me Jackie.
나를 Jackie라고 불러주세요.

7 My brother ________________ me that.
우리 형이 그것을 내게 말했다.

8 They ________________ Mike captain of their team.
그들은 Mike를 팀의 주장으로 뽑았다.

9 Tony ________________ this box useful.
Tony는 이 상자가 쓸모 있다고 여긴다.

10 I like to ________________ my room clean.
나는 내 방을 깨끗하게 유지하는 걸 좋아한다.

B 밑줄 친 부분을 바르게 고쳐 문장을 다시 쓰세요.

1 Please send to he the tickets.   그에게 티켓들을 보내세요.

➡ ____

2 She bought to he a bike for Christmas.   그녀는 그에게 크리스마스 선물로 자전거를 사 주었다.

➡ ____

3 Mom gave I a present.   엄마가 나에게 선물을 주었다.

➡ ____

4 Music makes happy me.   음악은 나를 행복하게 한다.

➡ ____

5 I don't find her attractively.   나는 그녀가 매력적이라고 생각하지 않는다.

➡ ____

6 It makes me nervously.   그것은 나를 불안하게 만든다.

➡ ____

7 They left open the door.   그들은 문을 열어 두었다.

➡ ____

8 Shopping makes tired me.   쇼핑은 나를 지치게 한다.

➡ ____

9 They proved he wrong.   그들은 그가 틀렸다는 것을 증명했다.

➡ ____

10 Tony finds her new book amazingly.   Tony는 그녀의 새 책이 굉장하다고 생각한다.

➡ ____

A 우리말과 같은 뜻이 되도록 주어진 말을 이용하여 문장을 완성하세요.

1 당신은 그녀에게 그 돈을 지불할 수 있나요? (pay)

→ Can you ______________ ______________ the money?

2 나는 그에게 그 사진들을 보여주지 않았다. (show)

→ I didn't ______________ ______________ the photos.

3 노래 부르기는 그녀를 행복하게 한다. (make, happy)

→ Singing ______________ ______________ ______________.

4 Jane은 그녀의 아들 이름을 David라고 지었다. (named, son)

→ Jane ______________ ______________ ______________ David.

5 Tony는 내게 점심을 사 주었다. (lunch, bought)

→ Tony ______________ ______________ ______________.

6 그는 나에게 이메일을 보냈다. (an email, sent)

→ He ______________ ______________ ______________ ______________.

7 그녀의 친구들은 그녀를 Kitty라고 부른다. (call, Kitty)

→ Her friends ______________ ______________ ______________.

8 그는 방을 깨끗하게 해 놓니? (the room, clean, keep)

→ Does he ______________ ______________ ______________ ______________?

9 나는 그에게 지금 질문을 하고 싶다. (a question, ask)

→ I want to ______________ ______________ ______________ ______________ now.

10 그들은 그에게 좋은 일자리를 제안했다. (a good job, offered)

→ They ______________ ______________ ______________ ______________ ______________.

11 그 영화는 나를 졸리게 한다. (makes, sleepy)

→ The movie ______________ ______________ ______________.

12 나는 그녀에게 지금 부탁을 하고 싶다. (a favor)

→ ____

13 나는 그에게 메시지를 보여주지 않았다. (the message)

→ ____

14 Tony는 내게 펜을 사 주었다. (a pen)

→ ____

15 Jane은 그녀의 딸 이름을 Amy라고 지었다. (her daughter)

→ ____

16 그는 나에게 선물을 보냈다. (a gift)

→ ____

17 그 영화는 나를 행복하게 한다. (makes, happy)

→ ____

MEMO

MEMO

# MEMO

MEMO

MEMO

초등 Grammar Inside

Workbook